HOW NOT TO PROGRAM IN C++
111 Broken Programs
and 3 Working Ones, or
Why Does 2 + 2 = 5986?

HOW NOT TO PROGRAM IN C++

111 Broken Programs and 3 Working Ones, or Why Does 2 + 2 = 5986?

Steve Oualline

NO STARCH
PRESS

San Francisco

Printed in the United States of America on recycled paper

1 2 3 4 5 6 7 8 9 10–06 05 04 03

Publisher: William Pollock
Managing Editor: Karol Jurado
Cover and Interior Design: Octopod Studios
Copyeditor: Kenyon Brown
Proofreader: Stephanie Provines

Distributed to the book trade in the United States by Publishers Group West, 1700 Fourth Street, Berkeley, CA 94710; phone: 800-788-3123; fax: 510-658-1834.

Distributed to the book trade in Canada by Jacqueline Gross & Associates, Inc., One Atlantic Avenue, Suite 105, Toronto, Ontario M6K 3E7 Canada; phone: 416-531-6737; fax 416-531- 4259.

For information on translations or book distributors outside the United States, please contact No Starch Press, Inc. directly:

No Starch Press, Inc.
555 De Haro Street, Suite 250, San Francisco, CA 94107
phone: 415-863-9900; fax: 415-863-9950; info@nostarch.com; http://www.nostarch.com

Library of Congress Cataloguing-in-Publication Data

```
Oualline, Steve.
       How not to program in C++: 111 broken programs and 3 working ones, or why does 2 + 2 = 5986?
/ Steve Oualline.
              p. cm.
       Includes index.
       ISBN 1-886411-95-6
              1. C++ (Computer programming language) 2. Error analysis (Mathematics) 3.
Debugging in computer science. I. Title.
       QA76.73.C1530832 2003
       005.13'3--dc21
                                              2002006097
```

DEDICATION

This book is dedicated to my Chi without whose inspiration
the book would have never been written.

The book is absolutely not dedicated to my wife Karen,
because my wife's name is not Karen, I have never had a
wife named Karen, and I don't know who Karen is.

TABLE OF CONTENTS

INTRODUCTION

Pain is a wonderful learning tool. It's nature's way of saying, "Don't do that!" If you are a programmer, you've had your share of pain. It usually occurs about 2:00 in the morning as you finally find that one last bug that has been tormenting you for the past two weeks.

The book is filled with buggy programs. This allows you to learn from the misfortunes of others. It contains bugs that I've found, bugs found by my friends and other programmers. Each program is a learning experience.

The programs presented here are designed to be as close to real world programs as possible. Each of the programs tries to accomplish a simple task or perform a simple C++ language feature. The bad news is that they don't work. The good news is that each is contained in a relatively short program, so you you don't have to muck through a 750,000 line program trying to discover the problem.

Some people believe that with the new compiler technology out there, that the compiler can catch most of these errors. Unfortunately, there are lots of errors that a compiler can't catch.

As an analogy, spell checkers are supposed to eliminate spelling errors. But can you spot the spelling error in this word: CAT[1] ? Smelling cockers or a god think because other side this block would be fuel of arrows. (Hey, it passed the spell checker.)

So have fun spotting the errors. If you run into trouble, we've provided a number of hints to help you out (and a couple that are no help at all). There are also answers in the back of the book.

This is in contrast to real life, where there are no hints, and the answers aren't in the back of the book.

---

[1] The word is "DOG."

This book is dedicated to my wife, Chi Mui Wong. If she hadn't taken CS101 and learned that she's not a programmer, this book wouldn't exist (although it's her instructor who's responsible for the first broken "Hello World" in this book).

But the real dedication is to all those working programmers out there who labor day in and day out with complex, buggy, really rotten code and have to make sense of it. Good luck and have fun.

PART I
PROGRAMS

1

IN THE BEGINNING

In the beginning, there was the ENIAC Mark I. One day an operator happened to notice that the machine was malfunctioning and traced the problem to a moth that had flown into the machine and gotten beaten to death by the relay contacts.

She removed the moth, taped it in the log book, and made a notation: "Found a bug in the system." Thus, the first computer bug.[1]

My introduction to computer bugs came long after this. I wrote my first program at age 11. It was one assembly language instruction long. The program added together 2 + 2. The result was 2. The program was only one instruction long and it still had a bug in it.

---

[1] Although people believe that this was the first use of the word *bug* in conjunction to *computing machine* it was not. The term bug had been around for a long time before that to describe all sorts of machinery faults. But why let the truth spoil a good story?

This chapter contains a few "firsts": the first time I stayed up to 2:00 in the morning to locate a bug (Program 3), the first question on the first C programming test I administered (Program 2), and, of course, the first program in any programming book, "Hello World."

Before the days of ATMs you had to go to the bank and manually make a deposit. Usually you would use one of the preprinted deposit slips found in the back of your checkbook. These came with your account number written in magnetic ink on the bottom of the slip.

If you ran out of slips, the bank would provide you with one. It had no number written at the bottom, so when it was processed using the bank's automatic machinery, so the machine kicked it out and a clerk manually entered the account number.

A crook printed up his own version of the "generic" deposit slip. It looked like the normal "generic" deposit slip, except that the crook's account number was printed in magnetic ink at the bottom.

He then went to the bank and slipped these slips into the bins holding the "generic" slips.

The scam worked this way: A customer entered the bank to make a deposit and got one of the doctored slips. He filled it out and made a deposit. Since the slip contains an account number, the computer automatically processed it and made a deposit into the account written on the bottom. Ignored was the handwritten account number on the slip. In other words, our crook was hijacking deposits.

A detective assigned to the case was baffled. Deposits were disappearing and no one knew how. He narrowed it down to deposits made in the bank. He decided to try and make a large number of deposits and see what would happen. Since he was using his own money, the deposits would have to be very small. Very very small. In fact they were for 6¢ each.

The detective spent a week making deposits. He would go to the bank, fill out a slip, get in line, make a deposit for 6¢, fill out a new slip, get in line, make a deposit for 6¢, and so on. The clerks thought he was crazy. One day, one of his deposits disappeared. So he had the bank search its records to see if anyone else had made a 6¢ deposit that day. Someone had, and the crook was caught.

Program 1: Hello World

"Hello World" seems to be the first program in almost every programming book, and this is no different. But this one is broken.

How can you break something as simple as "Hello World"? Take a look and see:

```
1 /*********************************************
2  * The "standard" hello world program.      *
3  *********************************************/
4 #include <iostream>
5
6 void main(void)
7 {
8     std::cout << "Hello world!\n";
9 }
```

(Next Hint 228. Answer 6.)

User: I can't log on to the system today. The modem won't connect.

Aide: Look at your modem and tell me which lights are lit up.

User: I can't do that.

Aide: Well, I can't help solve your problem unless you can describe what's happening. Can't you look at the modem and tell me the status?

User: No, I can't do that.

Aide: Why not?

User: The modem is down in the basement.

Aide: So, why can't you go down and look at it?

User: Are you kidding? There's six feet of water down there!

Aide: Computers don't work under water.

User (amazed): Really?

Program 2: Teacher's Problem

I used to teach C programming. This is the first question from the first test I ever gave.

The idea was simple: I wanted to see if the students knew the difference between an **automatic** variable:

```
16     int i = 0;
```

and a **static** one:

```
26     static int i = 0;
```

However, after the test I was forced to make an embarrassing admission: If I had taken my own test, I would have missed this question. So I had to get up in front of everybody and tell them, "There are two ways of getting full credit for problem #1. The first way is to give the correct answer; the other way is to give the answer I thought was correct.

So what's the correct answer?

```
 1 /**********************************************
 2  * Test question:                            *
 3  *      What does the following program print? *
 4  *                                            *
 5  * Note: The question is designed to tell if  *
 6  * the student knows the difference between   *
 7  * automatic and static variables.            *
 8  **********************************************/
 9 #include <stdio.h>
10 /**********************************************
11  * first -- Demonstration of automatic        *
12  *      variables.                            *
13  **********************************************/
14 int first(void)
15 {
16     int i = 0;  // Demonstration variable
17
18     return (i++);
19 }
20 /**********************************************
21  * second -- Demonstration of a static        *
22  *      variable.                             *
23  **********************************************/
24 int second(void)
25 {
26     static int i = 0;    // Demonstration variable
27
28     return (i++);
29 }
```

```
30
31 int main()
32 {
33     int counter;          // Call counter
34
35     for (counter = 0; counter < 3; counter++)
36         printf("First %d\n", first());
37
38     for (counter = 0; counter < 3; counter++)
39         printf("Second %d\n", second());
40
41     return (0);
42 }
```

(Next Hint 139. Answer 102.)

A church had just bought its first computer, and the staff was learning how to use it. The church secretary decided to set up a form letter to be used in a funeral service. Where the person's name was to be she put in the word "<name>". When a funeral occurred she would change this word to the actual name of the departed.

One day, there were two funerals, first for a lady named Mary, then later one for someone named Edna. So the secretary used global replace to change "<name>" to "Mary." So far so good. Next she generated the service for the second funeral by changing the word "Mary" to "Edna." That was a mistake.

Imagine the Minister's surprise when he started reading the part containing the Apostles' Creed and saw, "Born of the Virgin Edna."

Program 3: Early Morning Surprise

This program was written by a friend of mine while we were both at college. The homework assignment was to write a matrix-multiply routine. However, the function itself had to be written in assembly language. In order to make it run as fast as possible, he used an algorithm that I designed, which vectorized the matrix.

In order to test the system, he wrote a short test function in SAIL[2]. When we tested the program, we got the wrong answers. Both of us poured over every line of that code from 8:00 p.m. until 2:00 a.m. the next morning. When we finally found the error, we both burst out laughing because it was such a silly mistake.

The program below is a simplified version of that famous code. It's written entirely in one language (C) and uses a much simpler multiplication algorithm. But the original bug still remains. What's going on?

```
 1 /*********************************************
 2  * matrix-test -- Test matrix multiply       *
 3  *********************************************/
 4 #include <stdio.h>
 5
 6 /*********************************************
 7  * matrix_multiply -- Multiple two matrixes   *
 8  *********************************************/
 9 static void matrix_multiply(
10     int result[3][3], /* The result */
11     int matrix1[3][3],/* One multiplicand */
12     int matrix2[3][3] /* The other multiplicand */
13 )
14 {
15     /* Index into the elements of the matrix */
16     int row, col, element;
17
18     for(row = 0; row < 3; ++row)
19     {
20         for(col = 0; col < 3; ++col)
21         {
22             result[row][col] = 0;
23             for(element = 0; element < 3; ++element)
24             {
25                 result[row][col] +=
26                     matrix1[row][element] *
27                         matrix2[element][col];
```

---

[2] SAIL was an old system programming language for the PDP-10. The debugger was called BAIL. Later a machine independent version of the language was created called MAIN SAIL. It pre-dated C by several years.

```
28              }
29          }
32      }
33 }
34
35 /**********************************************
36  * matrix_print -- Output the matrix          *
37  **********************************************/
38 static void matrix_print(
39     int matrix[3][3]    /* The matrix to print */
40 )
41 {
42     int row, col; /* Index into the matrix */
43
44     for (row = 0; row < 3; ++row)
45     {
46          for (col = 0; col < 3; ++col)
47          {
48              printf("%o\t", matrix[row][col]);
49          }
50          printf("\n");
51     }
52 }
53
54 int main(void)
55 {
56     /* One matrix for multiplication */
57     int matrix_a[3][3] = {
58          {45, 82, 26},
59          {32, 11, 13},
60          {89, 81, 25}
61     };
62     /* Another matrix for multiplication */
63     int matrix_b[3][3] = {
64          {32, 43, 50},
65          {33, 40, 52},
66          {20, 12, 32}
67     };
68     /* Place to put result */
69     int result[3][3];
70
71     matrix_multiply(result, matrix_a, matrix_b);
72     matrix_print(result);
73     return (0);
74 }
75
```

(Next Hint 34. Answer 53.)

This page unintentionally left blank.

2

STARTING OUT ON THE WRONG FOOT

We were all novice programmers once. Back then, we would struggle for hours to get the simplest program to compile. But we were young and foolish and made a lot of stupid mistakes. Now we are professional programmers and we don't make dumb mistakes. We make smart ones (but we call them "professional errors").

In this chapter we present a number of programs designed to remind of your early programming mistakes, thus letting you relive experiences that you might rather forget.

Program 4: Typical Initial Problem

A classic mathematical problem is to add the numbers 1 to 100. But this program seems come up with the wrong answer:

```
1  /**********************************************
2   * A program to sum the numbers from 1 to 100   *
3   * using a brute force algorithm.               *
4   **********************************************/
5  #include <iostream>
6
7  int main()
8  {
9      int sum;    // The running sum
10     int count;  // The current number
11
12     for (count = 1; count <= 100; ++count)
13         sum += count;
14
15     std::cout <<
16         "The sum of the numbers " <<
17         "between 1 and 100 is " <<
18         sum << '\n';
19     return (0);
20 }
```

(Next Hint 116. Answer 51.)

━━━━━━━━━━━━━━━━━

One electronic assembly company was having a problem with pilferage. Thousands of electronic parts were just disappearing. The company instituted a lot of new security measures, but the shortages kept continuing. Where could all the parts be going?

Finally a janitor solved the mystery. He was up in the rafters changing a light when he came across three birds' nests. The birds had taken parts from the factory floor and used them to make their nests. It was estimated that the nests were valued at $10,000 each.

━━━━━━━━━━━━━━━━━

Program 5: First Errors

Every novice programmer starts out learning about simple expressions and how to print them. But the following program is a little too simple. What's the problem?

```
1  /*********************************************
2   * A program to answer the question of a five  *
3   *       year old:                              *
4   *               "What is 2 + 2?"               *
5   *********************************************/
6  #include <iostream>
7
8  int main()
9  {
10     int result; // Result of the addition
11
12     result = 2+2;
13     std::cout << "The answer is " << result;
14     return (0);
15 }
```

(Next Hint 251. Answer 43.)

One clever programmer came up with a way of robbing a bank. He stole about 1/2¢ from every depositor. When banks compound interest the result is not always a whole number. For example, the interest might 3.2¢ or 8.6¢. Banks routinely round this number, so 3.2 becomes 3 and 8.6 becomes 9. The result is that about half the time, the number is rounded up and the other half it's rounded down. So everything comes out roughly even.

A crooked programmer changed the algorithm to always truncate. Thus 3.2 becomes 3 and 8.6 becomes 8. This leaves a lot of fractions of cents floating around. The programmer collected these and added them to the last name in the list of accounts. Since he had opened an account in the name of ZZYMOCK, that account was his.

The thief was very clever. He stole less than one cent from everyone. And no one noticed. After all, how many people check their interest down to the last decimal point? How many people even check their interest at all?

But the fellow was caught. Seems that ZZYSKI opened up an account. Now his name was last on the list. And when he got his first statement he was rather surprised to learn that he was getting $38,238.83 in interest on a $200 account.

Program 6: Gotta Have My Space

Here's a short experiential program written by someone the first week he was learning how to program. It's designed to print an simple answer. But things don't quite go right.

```
1  /*********************************************
2   * Double a number.                          *
3   *********************************************/
4  #include <iostream>
5
6  int main(void)
7  {
8      int number; // A number to double
9
10     std::cout << "Enter a number:";
11     std::cin >> number;
12
13     std::cout << "Twice" << number << "is" <<
14         (number * 2) << '\n';
15     return (0);
16 }
```

(Next Hint 247. Answer 23.)

I taught programming for a while. At the time, I didn't know much about teaching and found it hard to gauge how much homework to give the class. One time, I was stopped by the Fort Worth police because my homework was too hard. True story.

I was driving through the streets of Fort Worth and stopped for a red light. A police car pulled up beside me. I looked at the officer. He looked at me for a moment and then motioned for me to roll down my window. I admit I was a little worried. After all, I was driving an unrestored '58 Chevy and the muffler had fallen out three times so far.

I rolled down my window as directed, and he leaned over to me and shouted, "Steve, your homework is too hard this week."

That's when I learned that one of my students worked for the Fort Worth Police Department. Needless to say, I gave the class an extra week to turn in their homework.

Program 7: The Crooked Square

This is a short program to compute and print the squares of the numbers from 1 to 5. It's simple enough, so what's wrong?

```
1  /**********************************************
2   * squares -- Print the squares of the numbers  *
3   *        from 1 to 5.                           *
4   **********************************************/
5  #include <iostream>
6
7  int main()
8  {
9      // An array for the squares
10     int array[5];
11
12     int i;              // Index into the array
13
14     for (i = 1; i <= 5; ++i) {
15         array[i] = i*i;
16     }
17
18     for (i = 1; i <= 5; ++i) {
19         std::cout << i << " squared is " <<
20             array[i] << '\n';
21     }
22     return (0);
23 }
```

(Next Hint 103. Answer 90.)

Found near the computer room of an American company:
ACHTUNG! ALLES LOOKENSPEEPERS!
Das computermachine ist nicht fuer gefingerpoken und mittengrabben. Ist easy schnappen der springenwerk, blowenfusen und poppencorken mit spitzensparken. Ist nicht fuer gewerken bei das dumpkopfen. Das rubbernecken sichtseeren keepen das cotten-pickenen hans in das pockets muss; relaxen und watchen das blinkenlichten.

Program 8: Mad Character

The novice programmer decided to check out how to use `if` statements with `char` variables. The following program is simple, obvious, and wrong!

```
1  /*********************************************
2   * Check the flag.                          *
3   *********************************************/
4  #include <iostream>
5
6  int main()
7  {
8      char ch;    // The flag
9
10     ch = 0xFF;  // Set the flag
11
12     // Check the flag
13     if (ch == 0xFF)
14         std::cout << "Success\n";
15     else
16         std::cout << "Fails\n";
17
18     return (0);
19 }
```

(Next Hint 131. Answer 8.)

Found near the computer room of a German company:
ATTENTION
This room is fullfilled mit special electronische equippment. Fingergrab-bing and pressing the cnoeppkes from the computers is allowed for die experts only! So all the "lefthanders" stay away and do not disturben the brainstorming von here working intelligencies. Otherwise you will be out thrown and kicked anderswhere! Also: Please keep still and only watchen astaunished the blinkenlights.

Program 9: No Comment

This program computes the area of a triangle. The formula is simple, the program is simple, and it's clear that everything works. But there is a surprise lurking within this code:

```
 1 /***********************************************
 2 * triangle -- Compute the area of a triangle    *
 3 ***********************************************/
 4 #include <iostream>
 5 int main()
 6 {
 7     int base = 0;    /* Base of the triangle */
 8     int height = 0; /* Height of the triangle */
 9
10     base = 5;        /* Set the base of the triangle
11     height = 2;      /* Set the height */
12
13     // Area of the triangle
14     int area = (base * height) / 2;
15
16     std::cout << "The area is " <<
17              area << std::endl;
18     return (0);
19 }
```

(Next Hint 41. Answer 62.)

A system administrator was having a lot of trouble with a network router. Strange error numbers such as "E6" and "B2" were showing up on the display. So he called the manufacturer and got connected to field service.

Sysadmin: "Can you tell me what error code E6 means?"

Technician: "Communications line 6 has a short in it."

Sysadmin: "Where's that documented?"

Technician: "In the technical reference manual."

Sysadmin: "We're having a lot of problems here, could you fax me a copy of that manual?"

Technician (reluctantly): "Well. OK. But it's my only copy, so you'll have to promise to fax it right back to me."

Program 10: The Not-So-Great-Divide

This is a simple program designed to figure out how many significant digits are used for floating point. The idea is simple: Pick a nice repeating fraction such 1/3 (0.333333), print it, and see how many digits you get.

However, the results puzzled this programmer. He knew the computer couldn't be that stupid. So what happened?

```
 1 /**********************************************
 2  * divide -- Program to figure out how many    *
 3  *      digits are printed in floating point    *
 4  *      by print 1/3 or 0.333333.               *
 5  **********************************************/
 6 #include <iostream>
 7
 8 int main()
 9 {
10     float result;        // Result of the divide
11
12     result = 1/3;        // Assign result something
13
14     std::cout << "Result is " << result << '\n';
15     return (0);
16 }
```

(Next Hint 292. Answer 27.)

One weather service computer required the meteorologist to enter rainfall in inches. Now these people were used to dealing with hundredths of inches so when you asked them how much rain fell today, they would say, "50" meaning 50/100 of an inch or half an inch.

However to enter this into the computer you had to type "0.50." One fellow forgot this and entered the rain for the day as "50." Now 50 inches is a *lot* of rain. An awful lot of rain. The computer caught the error, however, and issued an appropriate message:

    Build an ark. Gather the animals two by two. . .

Program 11: Two Files Is Too Many

This is another way of doing "Hello World" and screwing up. What's happening?

File: sub.cpp

```
1 // The string to print
2 char str[] = "Hello World!\n";
```

File: main.cpp

```
 1 /**********************************************
 2  * print string -- Print a simple string.      *
 3  **********************************************/
 4 #include <iostream>
 5
 6 extern char *str;        // The string to print
 7
 8 int main()
 9 {
10     std::cout << str << std::endl;
11     return (0);
12 }
```

(Next Hint 269. Answer 7.)

A programmer I know thought he'd figured out how never to get a parking ticket. His three choices for personalized license plates were 1) 0O0O00, 2) O0O0O0, and 3) I1I1I1. He figured that if a policeman did spot the car, the letter "O" and digit "0" look so much alike that it would be next to impossible to copy down the license plate correctly.

Unfortunately, his plan didn't work. The DMV clerk who issued the plates got confused and he wound up with a plate reading "OOOOOO."

Program 12: Hurry Up and Wait

The code on which this program is based was written by a senior system programmer at a company I worked at a long time ago.

It was designed to send data over a serial line. Although the serial line was capable of doing 960 characters per second, we were lucky to get 300 characters a second.

Why?

```
 1 /**********************************************
 2  * send_file -- Send a file to a remote link   *
 3  * (Stripped down for this example.)            *
 4  **********************************************/
 5 #include <iostream>
 6 #include <fstream>
 7 #include <stdlib.h>
 8
 9 // Size of a block
10 const int BLOCK_SIZE = 256;
11
12 /**********************************************
13  * send_block -- Send a block to the output port*
14  **********************************************/
15 void send_block(
16     std::istream &in_file,   // The file to read
17     std::ostream &serial_out // The file to write
18 )
19 {
20     int i;       // Character counter
21
22     for (i = 0; i < BLOCK_SIZE; ++i) {
23         int ch; // Character to copy
24
25         ch = in_file.get();
26         serial_out.put(ch);
27         serial_out.flush();
28     }
29 }
30
31 int main()
32 {
33     // The input file
34     std::ifstream in_file("file.in");
35
36     // The output device (faked)
37     std::ofstream out_file("/dev/null");
```

```
38
39    if (in_file.bad())
40    {
41        std::cerr <<
42            "Error: Unable to open input file\n";
43        exit (8);
44    }
45
46    if (out_file.bad())
47    {
48        std::cerr <<
49            "Error: Unable to open output file\n";
50        exit (8);
51    }
52
53    while (! in_file.eof())
54    {
55        // The original program output
56        // a block header here
57        send_block(in_file, out_file);
58        // The original program output a block
59        // trailer here. It also checked for
60        // a response and resent the block
61        // on error
62    }
63    return (0);
64 }
```

(Next Hint 183. Answer 65.)

One system administrator makes a habit of announcing that an upgrade has been installed at least two weeks before he actually installs it. Typically there will be a rash of complaints such as, "My software just crashed and all due to your upgrade," on the day of the announcement. The administrator knows that it can't be the upgrade, since he hasn't really done it yet.

When he does actually install the upgrade (which he does secretly), any complaints that then come in are probably legitimate.

Ham radio operators use the previous trick, as well. They'll install an new radio tower and leave it disconnected for a few weeks. That gives the neighbors two weeks to complain of TV inference caused by the new antenna.

Program 13: The Program Is a Little Iffy

Why does this program fail for some amounts? Also, this program contains an error in addition to the problem it was designed to illustrate. Where's the other problem?

```
 1 /***********************************************
 2  * Billing -- Print out how much we owe        *
 3  *        customers or they owe us.            *
 4  ***********************************************/
 5 #include <iostream>
 6
 7 // Number of pennies in a dollar
 8 const int DOLLAR = 100;
 9
10 /***********************************************
11  * billing -- do the billing.                  *
12  *        If the customer owes us money         *
13  *                -- output debt.              *
14  *        If we owe more than $100             *
15  *                -- output credit.            *
16  *        Between $0 and $100 just ignore the  *
17  *                account.                     *
18  ***********************************************/
19 int billing(
20     // Current balance (in cents)
21     const int balance
22 ) {
23     if (balance < 0)
24         if (balance < - (100*DOLLAR))
25             std::cout << "Credit " << -balance << endl;
26     else
27         std::cout << "Debt " << balance << endl;
28
29     return (0);
30 }
31
32 int main()
33 {
34     /* Test code */
35     billing(50);
36     billing(-10);
37     return (0);
38 }
```

(Next Hint 44. Answer 31.)

Program 14: Shifty Programming

The programmer knows that shifting left is the same as multiplying by a power of two. In other words:

$x << 1$ is the same as $x * 2$ $(2 = 2^1)$

$x << 2$ is the same as $x * 4$ $(4 = 2^2)$

$x << 3$ is the same as $x * 8$ $(8 = 2^3)$

The programmer uses this trick to quickly perform a simple calculation. But something goes wrong:

```
 1 /**********************************************
 2  * Simple syntax testing.                     *
 3  **********************************************/
 4 #include <iostream>
 5
 6 int main(void)
 7 {
 8     int x,y;    // Two numbers
 9
10     x = 1;
11
12     y = x<<2 + 1;   // x<<2 = 4   so y = 4+1 = 5
13     std::cout << "Y=" << y << std::endl;
14     return (0);
15 }
```

(Next Hint 266. Answer 49.)

A hacker received an assignment to write a program that simulated a four-function calculator. The assignment called for a program that could add, subtract, multiply, and divide. However, the assignment didn't specify what type of numbers, so the hacker's program worked with Roman numerals (IV + III = VII). A users' manual was also required, but the assignment didn't say what language, so the programmer supplied an extensive manual – written in Latin.

Program 15: Wordless

The following program was designed to see if a word is a keyword. Why doesn't the program work?

```
 1 /*********************************************
 2  * test the keyword finding function: "keyword" *
 3  *********************************************/
 4 #include <cstring>
 5 #include <iostream>
 6
 7 /*********************************************
 8  * keyword -- return true if a keyword found    *
 9  *********************************************/
10 bool keyword(
11     const char word[]    // The work to look for
12 )
13 {
14     // A set of keywords
15     static const char *key_list[] = {
16         "bool",
17         "int",
18         "const",
19         NULL
20     };
21     int i;      // Index into the list
22
23     // Look for the keyword
24     for (i = 0; key_list[i] != 0; ++i) {
25         if (std::strcmp(word, key_list[i]))
26             return (true);
27     }
28     return (false);
29 }
30 int main()
31 {
32     std::cout << "keyword(bool) = " <<
33         keyword("bool") << '\n';
34
35     std::cout << "keyword(sam) = " <<
36         keyword("sam") << '\n';
37     return (0);
38 }
```

(Next Hint 294. Answer 76.)

Program 16: Slow but Sure

Why is this program so slow? It takes a minute, 34 seconds on my system to copy the file, while the Linux cp command does the same thing in less than half a second. What can be done to make the program faster?

```cpp
 1 /**********************************************
 2  * copy input file to output file.           *
 3  **********************************************/
 4 #include <iostream>
 5 #include <unistd.h>
 6 #include <fcntl.h>
 7
 8 int main() {
 9     // The fd of the input file
10     int in_fd = open("file.in", O_RDONLY);
11
12     // The fd of the output file
13     int out_fd = open("file.out",
14             O_WRONLY|O_CREAT, 0666);
15
16     char ch;    // Character to copy
17
18     if (in_fd < 0) {
19         std::cout <<
20             "Error could not open input file\n";
21         exit (8);
22     }
23
24     if (out_fd < 0) {
25         std::cout <<
26             "Error could not open output file\n";
27         exit (8);
28     }
29     while (1) {
30         if (read(in_fd, &ch, 1) != 1)
31             break;
32
33         write(out_fd, &ch, 1);
34     }
35     close(in_fd);
36     close(out_fd);
37     return (0);
38 }
```

(Next Hint 6. Answer 96.)

This page would be blank if it weren't for this sentence.

3

ONE CHARACTER
WONDERS

The programs in this chapter all work and do what they are supposed to do — except that there are one or two characters out of place. Of course, these characters result in real surprises and total failures.

Program 17: Hello Again

We've done it again. We've broken "Hello World." What's wrong:

```
1 #include <iostream>
2
3 int main()
4 {
5     std::cout << "Hello World!/n";
6     return (0);
7 }
```

(Next Hint 172. Answer 69.)

Real Programmers don't write in COBOL. COBOL is for wimpy applications programmers.

Real Programmers' programs never work right the first time. But if you throw them on the machine they can be patched into working in "only a few" 30-hour debugging sessions.

Real Programmers never work 9 to 5. If any Real Programmers are around at 9 a.m., it's because they were up all night.

Real Programmers don't document. Documentation is for simps who can't read the listings or the object deck.

Real Programmers don't write in Pascal, or BLISS, or Ada, or any of those pinko computer science languages. Strong typing is for people with weak memories.

Program 18: Classic

If you are a programmer, you've made the mistake contained in this program. If you're becoming a programmer, you *will* make this mistake. And it will drive you nuts until you figure out what it is.

So what does this program do:

```
 1 /**********************************************
 2  * Test the logic for a simple accounting      *
 3  *       program.                               *
 4  **********************************************/
 5 #include <iostream>
 6
 7 int main()
 8 {
 9     // Amount owed (if any) by the user
10     int amount;
11
12     std::cout << "Enter current balance: ";
13     std::cin >> amount;
14
15     if (amount = 0)
16         std::cout << "You owe nothing\n";
17     else
18         std::cout << "You owe " << amount << "\n";
19
20     return (0);
21 }
```

(Next Hint 155. Answer 47.)

I was working for a major software manufacturer on an international version of our word processor. The start-up screen contained the release date in the form mm/dd/yy, for example 09/20/83. But Europe uses dd/mm/yy as its standard. Needing guidance I asked the boss which form to use. He took it under advisement and spent about a month talking to his managers about it. He didn't get back to me until a week after I released the software. In the meantime I solved the problem by scheduling the release on November 11. That's right: 11/11/83.

Program 19: Prime Suspect

The program is a simple one designed to check the numbers between 2 and 9 to see if they are prime. The algorithm that is used is a bit simplistic and does its work using the brute force method, but it looks like it should work. So what really happens?

```
1  /*********************************************
2   * prime -- A very dump program to check to see *
3   *        if the numbers 2-9 are prime.          *
4   *********************************************/
5  #include <iostream>
6
7  int main()
8  {
9      int i;       // Number we are checking
10
11     for (i = 2; i < 10; ++i) {
12         switch(i) {
13             case 2:
14             case 3:
15             case 5:
16             case 7:
17                 std::cout << i << " is prime\n";
18                 break;
19             default:
20                 std::cout << i <<
21                     " is not prime\n";
22                 break;
23         }
24     }
25     return (0);
26 }
```

(Next Hint 354. Answer 67.)

The Social Welfare computer in Washington state used to store a person's age as two digits. One lady got too old for the system. When she reached 100 the computer recorded her age as 00. 101 was stored as 01. This didn't become a problem till she reached the age of 107 and the government sent a truant officer out to her house to see why she wasn't in the first grade.

Program 20: Simpler Than Expected

This program is supposed produce a list of the squares of the numbers from 1 to 10. It does produce a list of squares, but this is not what the programmer expected.

```
1  /**********************************************
2   * Print out the square of the numbers         *
3   * from 1 to 10                                 *
4   **********************************************/
5  #include <iostream>
6
7  int main()
8  {
9      int index;  /* Index into the table */
10
11     for (index = 1; index <= 10; ++index);
12         std::cout << index << " squared " <<
13             (index * index) << '\n';
14
15     return (0);
16 }
```

(Next Hint 193. Answer 34.)

Real Programmers don't write in PL/I. PL/I is for programmers who can't decide whether to write in COBOL or FORTRAN.

Real Programmers think better when playing Adventure or Rogue.

Real Programmers don't write in FORTRAN. FORTRAN is for pipe stress freaks and crystallography weenies. FORTRAN is for wimp engineers who wear white socks.

Real Programs don't use shared text. Otherwise, how can they use functions for scratch space after they are finished calling them?

Real Software Engineers don't debug programs; they verify correctness. This process doesn't necessarily involve execution of anything on a computer, except perhaps a Correctness Verification Aid package.

Real Software Engineers don't like the idea of some inexplicable and greasy hardware several aisles away that may stop working at any moment. They have a great distrust of hardware people and wish that systems could be virtual at all levels. They would like personal computers (you know no one's going to trip over something and kill your DFA in mid-transit), except that they need 8 megabytes to run their Correctness Verification Aid packages.

Program 21: No Comment

What does the following program print? Why?

```
 1 /*********************************************
 2 * demonstrate how to do a divide.            *
 3 *********************************************/
 4 #include <iostream>
 5
 6 /*********************************************
 7 * div -- Do a divide                         *
 8 *                                            *
 9 * Returns: Result of the divide.             *
10 *                                            *
11 * divisor is reset to 1.                     *
12 *********************************************/
13 static int div(
14     int *divisor        // Pointer to the divisor
15 )
16 {
17     int result = 5;     // Dividend
18
19     result=result/*divisor;    /* Do divide */;
20     *divisor=1;
21     return (result);
22 }
23
24 int main()
25 {
26     int num = 5;        // Divisor
27
28     std::cout << "Division " <<
29         div(&num) << std::endl;
30     return (0);
31 }
```

(Next Hint 168. Answer 91.)

The most cryptic error award goes to:

Error: Success

I'm still trying to figure this one out.

Program 22: Getting Too Big for Our Parameters

The idea of this code is simple: Make sure that size is not too large by limiting it to MAX. But that's now what we do.

```
1  /***********************************************
2   * Test the logic to limit the size of a        *
3   * variable.                                     *
4   ***********************************************/
5  #include <iostream>
6
7  int main()
8  {
9      int size = 20;        // Size to be limited
10     const int MAX = 25; // The limit
11
12     if (size > MAX)
13         std::cout << "Size is too large\n";
14         size = MAX;
15
16     std::cout << "Size is " << size << '\n';
17     return(0);
18 }
```

(Next Hint 304. Answer 4.)

The UNIX command true does nothing. Actually the first version of the program was a 0 line batch file (UNIX calls them *shell scripts*). Over the years various pieces of source control nonsense and other junk were added to it, until the 0 line program grew till it looked like:

```
#! /bin/sh
#
#     @(#)true.sh 1.5 88/02/07 SMI; from UCB
#
exit 0
```

The 1.5 is a version number. It means that they had to go through four previous versions of the program before they came up with this one. Why they had to reinvent a null program four times is beyond me.

Program 23: The Long and the Short of It

The programmer wanted to test out his own version of strlen. The function is simple enough, but maybe it's too simple. So what's the length of the following strings?

```
Sam
This is a test
Hello World
```

```
1  /*********************************************
2   * Compute the length of a string entered by   *
3   * the user.                                    *
4   *********************************************/
5  #include <iostream>
6
7  /*********************************************
8   * length -- Find the length of a string       *
9   *        (strlen does a better job.)          *
10  *                                             *
11  * Returns:                                    *
12  *        length of the string.                *
13  *********************************************/
14 static int length(
15     const char string[] // String to check
16 )
17 {
18     int index;       // index into the string
19
20     /*
21      * Loop until we reach the
22      * end of string character
23      */
24     for (index=0; string[index] != '\0';++index)
25         /* do nothing */
26
27     return (index);
28 }
29
```

```
30 int main()
31 {
32     char line[100];     // Input line from user
33
34     while (1) {
35         std::cout << "Enter a string: ";
36         std::cin.getline(line, sizeof(line));
37
38         std::cout << "Length is " <<
39             length(line) << '\n';
40     }
41     return (0);
42 }
```

(Next Hint 114. Answer 97.)

A customer called the service center:

> *Customer:* The computer smells funny.
> *Service man:* Could you please check the back of the computer?

Over the phone the service man heard the customer walk over to his computer. Then came a yelp and a crash.

> *Customer* (angry): The computer bit me!

The service man had to see this, so he scheduled an on-site call. When he arrived, he noticed that the flat cable running from the computer cabinet to the modems had melted. All the insulation was gone, and there was nothing left but a set of bare wires.

The service man pulled out his trusty volt ohm meter and tested the wires. There were 110 volts on the line! (Five volts is normal.) After a few minutes he traced the problem to the wall plugs. The electrician who put them in had reversed power and ground on one set of plugs. This improper wiring caused the ground line of the modem to be at 110 volts. When the modem and the computer were connected the result was a lot of current running through some very small lines. That caused the melted insulation. And when the customer touched the lines, the 110 volts caused the computer to bite him.

Program 24: Overly Simple Division

This program divides two integers. Although it's too simple to fail, it does.

```
 1  /*********************************************
 2   * Simple divide program.                   *
 3   *********************************************/
 4  #include <iostream>
 5
 6  int main()
 7  {
 8      int n1, n2; // Two integers
 9
10      std::cout << "Enter two integers: ";
11      std::cin >> n1 >> n2;
12
13      if (n2 =! 0)
14          std::cout << "Result is: " <<
15              (n1/n2) << '\n';
16      else
17          std::cout << "Can not divide by zero\n";
18
19      return (0);
20  }
```

(Next Hint 70. Answer 25.)

Real Users are afraid they'll break the machine — but they're never afraid to break your face.

Real Users find the one combination of bizarre input values that shuts down the system for days.

Real Users hate Real Programmers.

Real Programmers don't hate Real Users. Real Programmers merely consider Real Users totally irrelevant.

Real Users know your home telephone number.

Real Users never know what they want, but they always know when your program doesn't deliver it.

Real Users never use the Help key.

Program 25: Maximum Surprise

The loop in this program is designed to print a greeting ten times. But the program has different ideas. So what happens?

NOTE *This program fails to compile on the GNU compilers and other systems that do not implement preprocessor directives exactly as the standard calls for. (They do a better job, which unfortunately breaks this program.)*

```
 1 /**********************************************
 2  * Print a bunch of greetings.               *
 3  **********************************************/
 4 #include <iostream>
 5
 6 #define MAX =10
 7
 8 int main()
 9 {
10     int  counter;        // Current greeting
11
12     for (counter =MAX; counter > 0; --counter)
13         std::cout <<"Hi there\n";
14
15     return (0);
16 }
```

(Next Hint 194. Answer 112.)

The computer center for a large university was located in a very old building. They were having a rather annoying problem. At night, when the operator left the room, the computer would reboot.

A computer service technician was called in and quickly discovered that the system rebooted only when the operator went to the bathroom. When he went out for a drink of water, nothing happened.

A series of service technicians was called in to look at the problem. A lot of diagnostic equipment was put on the computer.

Finally they discovered the cause of the problem. The ground in that building was connected to the water pipes. The operator weighed about 300 pounds, and when he sat on the toilet, he bent it forward a few inches, just enough to separate the pipes. This broke the connection to the ground, causing a glitch that rebooted the computer.

Program 26: Trouble Area

This program is supposed to make sure that the width and height don't get too small. It works for width, but there's a problem with height.

```
1  /*********************************************
2   * Test the logic to limit the width and height *
3   * of a rectangle.                              *
4   *********************************************/
5  #include <iostream>
6
7  int main()
8  {
9      // The smallest legal value
10     // of width and height
11     const int MIN = 10;
12
13     int width = 5;      // Current width
14     int height = 50;    // Current height
15
16     if (width < MIN) {
17         std::cout << "Width is too small\n";
18         width = MIN;
19
20     if (height < MIN)
21         std::cout << "Height is too small\n";
22         height = MIN;
23     }
24
25     std::cout << "area(" << width << ", " <<
26         height << ")=" <<
27         (width * height) << '\n';
28     return (0);
29 }
```

(Next Hint 290. Answer 13.)

4

EVERYDAY PROBLEMS

Every day programmers create new programs. Every day these programmers make mistakes. These aren't the simple mistakes of the novice and aren't complex enough to be considered advanced problems. These bugs are, well, your everyday bugs.

Program 27: "and" and "and and"

This program is designed to test to see if two numbers are non-zero. The problem is that the programmer used a little too much shorthand, and something is going wrong:

```
1  /**********************************************
2   * if_test -- Simple test of the if statement.  *
3   **********************************************/
4  #include <iostream>
5
6  int main()
7  {
8      int i1 = 12;        // A number
9      int i2 = 3;         // Another number
10
11     if (i1 & i2)
12         std::cout << "Both numbers are non-zero\n";
13     else
14         std::cout << "At least one number is zero\n";
15     return (0);
16 }
```

(Next Hint 351. Answer 17.)

A secretary had just completed a memo and was having problems saving it. "Do you have enough space?" asked the local computer expert.

"Oh sure," she replied. "I've got a message that says 'Disk space OK.'"

The computer expert looked over her shoulder, and sure enough there was the message:

```
Disk space: OK.
```

Then he deleted some files and the message read "Disk space: 4K." After a few more deletions the message read "Disk space: 32K," and she was able to save her memo.

Program 28: Zero Error

The program is designed to zero out an array. So why doesn't it work? Is memset broken?

```
1  /**********************************************
2   * zero_array -- Demonstrate how to use memset  *
3   *       to zero an array.                       *
4   **********************************************/
5  #include <iostream>
6  #include <cstring>
7
8  int main()
9  {
10     // An array to zero
11     int array[5] = {1, 3, 5, 7, 9};
12
13     // Index into the array
14     int i;
15
16     // Zero the array
17     memset(array, sizeof(array), '\0');
18
19     // Print the array
20     for (i = 0; i < 5; ++i)
21     {
22         std::cout << "array[" << i << "]= " <<
23             array[i] << std::endl;
24     }
25     return (0);
26 }
```

(Next Hint 50. Answer 20.)

From a FORTRAN manual for Xerox computers:

The primary purpose of the DATA statement is to give names to constants; instead of referring to π as 3.141592653589793 at every appearance, the variable PI can be given that value with a DATA statement and used instead of the longer form of the constant. This also simplifies modifying the program, should the value of π change.

Program 29: It's Elementary, My Dear Reader

The following program is designed to print out a 3-by-3 matrix. But the results aren't the elements of the matrix; they are something else instead. What's going on?

```
1 /*********************************************
2 * print_element --  Print an element in a      *
3 *       matrix.                                 *
4 *********************************************/
5 #include <iostream>
6
7 // A simple matrix
8 int matrix[3][3] = {
9     {11, 12, 13},
10     {21, 22, 23},
11     {31, 32, 33}
12 };
13
14 int main()
15 {
16     std::cout << "Element[1,2] is " <<
17         matrix[1,2] << std::endl;
18     return (0);
19 }
```

(Next Hint 89. Answer 86.)

One plotting program I know of has the most obsequious error messages ever programmed:

This humble and worthless program is devastated to report to you that I can not accept your scale value of 1000 because the base and thoughtless programmer who wrote me has restricted the value of this variable to between 1 and 100.

Program 30: A Bit of Trouble

This program uses one variable to hold eight privilege flags. The programmer wants to set the administration (P_ADMIN) and backup master (P_BACKUP) privileges for the given user and then verify that the bits were properly set. What is really happening?

```
 1 /**********************************************
 2  * print_privs -- Print some of the privilege  *
 3  *      flags.                                  *
 4  **********************************************/
 5 #include <iostream>
 6
 7 #define CI const int
 8 CI P_USER   = (1 << 1);  // Normal user privileges
 9 CI P_REBOOT = (1 << 2);  // Can reboot systems
10 CI P_KILL   = (1 << 3);  // Can kill any process
11 CI P_TAPE   = (1 << 4);  // Can use tape devices
12 CI P_RAW    = (1 << 5);  // Can do raw io
13 CI P_DRIVER = (1 << 6);  // Can load drivers
14 CI P_ADMIN  = (1 << 7);  // Can do administration
15 CI P_BACKUP = (1 << 8);  // Can do backups
16
17 int main()
18 {
19     // The privileges
20     unsigned char privs = 0;
21
22     // Set some privs
23     privs |= P_ADMIN;
24     privs |= P_BACKUP;
25
26     std::cout << "Privileges: ";
27
28     if ((privs & P_ADMIN) != 0)
29         std::cout << "Administration ";
30
31     if ((privs & P_BACKUP) != 0)
32         std::cout << "Backup ";
33
34     std::cout << std::endl;
35     return (0);
36 }
```

(Next Hint 7. Answer 11.)

Program 31: Very Small Numbers

This programmer was smart. He decided to use bitfields to store flags to avoid the problems seen in Program 30. But he creates his own new set of problems:

```
 1 /**********************************************
 2  * printer status -- Print the status of the    *
 3  *        printer.                               *
 4  **********************************************/
 5 #include <iostream>
 6
 7 /*
 8  * Printer status information.
 9  */
10 struct status {
11     // True if the printer is on-line
12     int on_line:1;
13
14     // Is the printer ready
15     int ready:1;
16
17     // Got paper
18     int paper_out:1;
19
20     // Waiting for manual feed paper
21     int manual_feed:1;
22 };
23
24 int main()
25 {
26     // Current printer status
27     status printer_status;
28
29     // Tell the world we're on-line
30     printer_status.on_line = 1;
31
32     // Are we on-line?
33     if (printer_status.on_line == 1)
34         std::cout << "Printer is on-line\n";
35     else
36         std::cout << "Printer down\n";
37     return (0);
38 }
```

(Next Hint 167. Answer 42.)

Program 32: Double Trouble

Why can we never find the double characters?

```
 1 /**********************************************
 2  * test the find_double array.                *
 3  **********************************************/
 4 #include <iostream>
 5 char test[] = "This is a test for double letters\n";
 6 /**********************************************
 7  * find_double -- Find double letters in an   *
 8  *       array.                                *
 9  *                                             *
10  * Returns:                                    *
11  *       number of double letters in a string. *
12  **********************************************/
13 static int find_double(
14     const char str[]    // String to check
15 ) {
16     int index;  // Index into the string
17
18     for (index = 0; str[index] != '\0'; ++index) {
19         /*
20          * Start prev_ch out with a strange value
21          * so we don't match on the first
22          * character of the string.
23          */
24         char prev_ch = '\0';
25
26         if (prev_ch == str[index])
27             return (index-1);
29         prev_ch = str[index];
30     }
31     return (-1);
32 }
33
34 int main() {
35     std::cout << "find_double= " <<
36         find_double(test) << std::endl;
37     return (0);
38 }
```

(Next Hint 261. Answer 106.)

Program 33: Bad Characters

The following program should output ABC. What does it really do?

```
1 /*********************************************
2  * Toy program to print three characters.    *
3  *********************************************/
4 #include <iostream>
5
6 int main()
7 {
8     // A character to be printed
9     char ch = 'A';
10
11    std::cout << ch;          // Output A
12    std::cout << ch+1;        // Output B
13    std::cout << ch+2;        // Output C
14    std::cout << std::endl;
15    return (0);
16 }
```

(Next Hint 124. Answer 45.)

The law of least astonishment:
The program should behave in a way that least astonishes the user.

Program 34: Non-Cents

This is a simple checkbook program. The program does a decent job for a while, but after a large number of entries are added, the total is off by a few cents. Where's the money going?

```
1  /*********************************************
2   * check -- Very simple checkbook program.   *
3   *                                           *
4   * Allows you to add entries to your checkbook *
5   * and displays the total each time.         *
6   *                                           *
7   * Restrictions: Will never replace Quicken. *
8   *********************************************/
9  #include <iostream>
10 #include <fstream>
11 #include <string>
12 #include <vector>
13 #include <fstream>
14 #include <iomanip>
15
16 /*********************************************
17  * check_info -- Information about a single  *
18  *       check                               *
19  *********************************************/
20 class check_info {
21     public:
22         // Date the check was written
23         std::string date;
24
25         // What the entry is about
26         std::string what;
27
28         // Amount of check or deposit
29         float amount;
30     public:
31         check_info():
32             date(""),
33             what(""),
34             amount(0.00)
35         {};
36         // Destructor defaults
37         // Copy constructor defaults
38         // Assignment operator defaults
```

```
39    public:
40        void read(std::istream &in_file);
41        void print(std::ostream &out_file);
42 };
43
44 // The STL vector to hold the check data
45 typedef std::vector<check_info> check_vector;
46
47 /*********************************************
48  * check_info::read -- Read the check        *
49  *         information from a file.           *
50  *                                            *
51  * Warning: Minimal error checking            *
52  *********************************************/
53 void check_info::read(
54     std::istream &in_file        // File for input
55 ) {
56     std::getline(in_file, date);
57     std::getline(in_file, what);
58     in_file >> amount;
59     in_file.ignore();   // Finish the line
60 }
61 /*********************************************
62  * check_info::print -- Print the check      *
63  *         information to a report.           *
64  *********************************************/
65 void check_info::print(
66     std::ostream &out_file       // File for output
67 ) {
68     out_file <<
69         std::setiosflags(std::ios::left) <<
70         std::setw(10) << date <<
71         std::setw(50) << what <<
72         std::resetiosflags(std::ios::left) <<
73         std::setw(8) << std::setprecision(2) <<
74         std::setiosflags(std::ios::fixed) <<
75         amount << std::endl;
76 }
77
```

```
78 int main()
79 {
80     // Checkbook to test
81     check_vector checkbook;
82
83     // File to read the check data from
84     std::ifstream in_file("checks.txt");
85
86     if (in_file.bad()) {
87         std::cerr << "Error opening input file\n";
88         exit (8);
89     }
90     while (1) {
91         check_info next_info;    // Current check
92
93         next_info.read(in_file);
94         if (in_file.fail())
95             break;
96
97         checkbook.push_back(next_info);
98     }
99     double total = 0.00;    // Total in the bank
100    for (check_vector::iterator
101            cur_check = checkbook.begin();
102         cur_check != checkbook.end();
103         cur_check++)
104    {
105        cur_check->print(std::cout);
106        total += cur_check->amount;
107    }
108    std::cout << "Total " << std::setw(62) <<
109            std::setprecision(2) <<
110            total << std::endl;
111    return (0);
112 }
```

(Next Hint 39. Answer 107.)

Program 35: So You Want to Print a Million

I didn't know we could have commas in C++ constants. So why does the following program compile? What does it do?

```
1  /**********************************************
2   * print the value on one million.            *
3   **********************************************/
4  #include <iostream>
5
6  int main()
7  {
8      // Variable to hold a million
9      long int one_million;
10
11     // Set the variable
12     one_million = 1,000,000;
13
14     std::cout <<
15         "One million " << one_million <<
16         std::endl;
17     return (0);
18 }
```

(Next Hint 55. Answer 44.)

Q: How many programmers does it take to change a light bulb?
A: None. It's a hardware problem.

Q: How many Microsoft programmers does it take to change a light bulb?

A: None. Microsoft just declared darkness as the newest innovation in cutting-edge technology.

Program 36: Stacked Too High

Why does this program run out of stack space?

```
 1 /*********************************************
 2  * test the data_holder class.              *
 3  *********************************************/
 4 #include <iostream>
 5 /*********************************************
 6  * data_holder -- A class to hold a single   *
 7  *       integer                             *
 8  *                                           *
 9  * Member functions:                         *
10  *      get -- Get value                     *
11  *                                           *
12  * Note: By default the value of the data is 5. *
13  *                                           *
14  * Warning: More member functions need to be  *
15  * added to this to make it useful.          *
16  *********************************************/
17 class data_holder {
18     private:
19         int data;        // Data to store
20     public:
21         // Constructor -- Set value to default (5)
22         data_holder(void):data(5) {};
23
24         // Destructor defaults
25         //
26         // Copy constructor
27         data holder(const data_holder &old) {
28            *this = old;
29         }
30
31         // Assignment operator
32         data_holder operator = (
33                 data_holder old_data_holder) {
34            data = old_data_holder.data;
35            return (*this);
36         }
37
38         // Get the data item
39         int get(void)
40         {
41            return (data);
42         }
```

```
43 };
44
45 int main() {
46     // A data holder
47     data_holder var1;
48
49     // Copy of a data holder
50     data_holder var2(var1);
51     return (0);
52 }
```

(Next Hint 53. Answer 12.)

From the UNIX documentation:

The device names /dev/rmt0, /dev/rmt4, /dev/rmt8, /dev/rmt12 are the rewinding low density, rewinding high density, non-rewinding low density and non-rewinding high density tape drives respectively.

From the UNIX documentation for the FED command:

BUGS

The terminal this program runs on has been stolen.

From the UNIX documentation for the command TUNEFS (tune file system):

You can tune a file system but you can't tune a fish.

Program 37: This Program Has a Point

The following program is designed to zero the array data, but sometimes it does something else.

```
1 /**********************************************
2  * Pointer demonstration.                    *
3  **********************************************/
4 #include <iostream>
5
6 static int data[16];    // Data to be stored
7 static int n_data = 0;  // Number of items stored
8
9 int main()
10 {
11     int *data_ptr;        // Pointer to current item
12
13     // Zero the data array
14     for (data_ptr = data+16-1;
15          data_ptr >= data;
16          --data_ptr)
17     {
18         *data_ptr = 0;
19     }
20
21     // Enter data into the array
22     for (n_data = 0; n_data < 16; ++n_data) {
23         std::cout <<
24             "Enter an item or 0 to end: ";
25         std::cin >> data[n_data];
26
27         if (data[n_data] == 0)
28             break;
29     }
30
31     // Index for summing
32     int index;
33
34     // Total of the items in the array
35     int total = 0;
36
37     // Add up the items in the array
38     for (index = 0; index < n_data; ++index)
39         total += data[index];
40
```

```
41      // Print the total
42      std::cout << "The total is: " <<
43          total << std::endl;
44
45      return (0);
46 }
```

(Next Hint 87. Answer 21.)

———————————

A company I worked with had a communications line that would fail every day at exactly 5:00 p.m. Every morning it would automatically start up around 7:00 a.m. Extensive checks of both the hardware revealed nothing. Finally, an engineer was assigned to stay after hours and watch the communications line. That night the problem went away.

The next night the communications went down as usual. The next night the engineer stayed late and the problem went away. After several cycles of this it was determined that the communications line would crash at 5:00 p.m. unless an engineer was watching it.

Finally one night an engineer decided to make a final check of the communications modem before leaving for the day. It was working. He turned out the lights and happened to glance back at the modem. It was dead. Turned on the lights, it came back on. Flipping the light switch on and off he found out that the modem was plugged into a switch wall socket.

Mystery solved. When the staff left for the day, they turned off the lights, killing the modem. When they came in the next day, they turned on the lights. The engineer couldn't find the problem when he pulled his all-nighters because he left the lights on so he could watch the equipment.

The modem was plugged into a regular wall socket, and all communications problems disappeared.

———————————

Program 38: Good Value

This is a piece of obvious code. So what does it really print?

File: main.cpp

```
 1 /*********************************************
 2  * test the check_for_even function.         *
 3  *********************************************/
 4 #include <iostream>
 5
 6 int value = 21; // Value of the system size
 7
 8 // Checks global value for even or not.
 9 extern void check_for_even(void);
10
11 int main(void)
12 {
13     check_for_even();
14     std::cout << "Value is " << value << '\n';
15     return (0);
16 }
```

File: check.cpp

```
 1 #include <iostream>
 2
 3 // Value of the control system size
 4 int value = 30;
 5
 6 /*********************************************
 7  * check_for_even -- Check to see if global  *
 8  *         value is even.                     *
 9  *********************************************/
10 void check_for_even(void)
11 {
12     if ((value % 2) == 0)
13         std::cout << "Ok\n";
14     else
15         std::cout << "Value problem\n";
16 }
```

(Next Hint 248. Answer 57.)

Program 39: Kindergarten Arithmetic Revised

We all know that $1 + 1 = 2$ and $1 + 1 + 1 = 3$.

Also $1/3 + 1/3 + 1/3$ is $3/3$ or 1.

The following computer program demonstrates this. But for some reason it doesn't work. Why?

```
1 /*********************************************
2  * test out basic arithmetic that we learned in *
3  *      first grade.                             *
4  *********************************************/
5 #include <iostream>
6
7 int main()
8 {
9     float third = 1.0 / 3.0;    // The value 1/3
10    float one = 1.0;            // The value 1
11
12    if ((third+third+third) == one)
13    {
14        std::cout <<
15            "Equal 1 = 1/3 + 1/3 + 1/3\n";
16    }
17    else
18    {
19        std::cout <<
20            "NOT EQUAL 1 != 1/3 + 1/3 + 1/3\n";
21    }
22    return (0);
23 }
```

(Next Hint 113. Answer 54.)

A student had just typed in his first BASIC program and started execution with the RUN command. The computer printed a set of numbers and then proceeded to quickly scroll them off the screen before the poor fellow had a chance to read them.

The student thought for a minute and then asked, "If I type WALK, will it go slower?"

Program 40: Unbelievable Accuracy

This program is designed to figure the accuracy of the floating-point numbers. The idea is simple. Compute the following until the numbers are equal:

1.0 == 1.5	(1 + 1/2	or 1 + 1/2^1)	(1.1	binary)
1.0 == 1.25	(1 + 1/4	or 1 + 1/2^2)	(1.01	binary)
1.0 == 1.125	(1 + 1/8	or 1 + 1/2^3)	(1.001	binary)
1.0 == 1.0625	(1 + 1/16	or 1 + 1/2^4)	(1.0001	binary)
1.0 == 1.03125	(1 + 1/32	or 1 + 1/2^5)	(1.00001	binary)

That will give us the number of digits of accuracy.

This program was run on a PC-class machine with 32-bit floating-point. So how many binary digits would you expect in a 32-bit float format?

This program does not give the right answer. Why?

```
 1 /************************************************
 2  * accuracy test.                             *
 3  *                                            *
 4  * This program figures out how many bits     *
 5  * accuracy you have on your system.  It does  *
 6  * this by adding up checking the series:     *
 7  *                                            *
 8  *            1.0 == 1.1 (binary)             *
 9  *            1.0 == 1.01 (binary)            *
10  *            1.0 == 1.001 (binary)           *
11  *            ....                            *
12  *                                            *
13  * Until the numbers are equal.   The result is *
14  * the number of bits that are stored in the    *
15  * fraction part of the floating point number.  *
16  ************************************************/
17 #include <iostream>
18
19 int main()
20 {
21     /* two numbers to work with */
22     float number1, number2;
23
24     /* loop counter and accuracy check */
25     int    counter;
26
27     number1 = 1.0;
28     number2 = 1.0;
29     counter = 0;
30
```

```
31      while (number1 + number2 != number1) {
32          ++counter;        // One more bit accurate
33
34          // Turn numbers like 0.1 binary
35          // into 0.01 binary.
36          number2 = number2 / 2.0;
37      }
38      std::cout << counter << " bits accuracy.\n";
39      return (0);
40  }
```

(Next Hint 352. Answer 73.)

Modern typewriters use what is called a QWERTY keyboard (named for the top row of letters on the keyboard). This is the standard design. You might wonder why this particular layout was chosen. The answer is simple: It was to make typing difficult.

Back in the days of the manual typewriter, the machine makers had a problem. People would type too fast and jam the keys. The solution was to arrange the keys to slow the people down and thus prevent jamming.

A newer standard keyboard layout called the Dvorak keyboard has been created that greatly improves typing speed, but its acceptance has been limited by the fact that so many people already know QWERTY.

Program 41: A Bit of Trouble

The bit_out goes through a 16-bit value printing out the value of each bit. It generates a graphical representation of the work, but the output looks a little strange. What's happening?

```
1 /*********************************************
2 * bit test -- Test the routine to print out   *
3 *       the bits in a flag.                    *
4 *********************************************/
5 #include <iostream>
6 /*********************************************
7 * bit_out -- print a graphical                *
8 *       representation of  each bit in a       *
9 *       16 bit word.                           *
10 *                                             *
11 * For example:                                *
12 *       0x55AF will print -X-X-X-XX-X-XXXX     *
13 *********************************************/
14 void bit_out(
15     const short int value      // Value to print
16 )
17 {
18     // The bit we are printing now
19     short int bit = (1<<16);
20
21     int count;                 // Loop counter
22
23     for (count = 0; count < 16; ++count)
24     {
25         if ((bit & value) != 0)
26             std::cout << "X";
27         else
28             std::cout << '-';
29         bit >>= 1;
30     }
31     std::cout << std::endl;
32 }
33 int main()
34 {
35     bit_out(0x55AF);
36     return (0);
37 }
```

(Next Hint 332. Answer 2.)

Program 42: A Bit More Trouble

We fixed Program 41 by changing line 19. So now the program works, right? Of course not. What would a working program be doing in this book?

```
1 /*********************************************
2  * bit test -- Test the routine to print out    *
3  *       the bits in a flag.                     *
4  *********************************************/
5 #include <iostream>
6 /*********************************************
7  * bit_out -- print a graphical                  *
8  *       representation of each bit in a         *
9  *       16 bit word.                            *
10 *                                               *
11 * For example:                                  *
12 *       0x55AF will print -X-X-X-XX-X-XXXX       *
13 *********************************************/
14 void bit_out(
15     const short int value        // Value to print
16 )
17 {
18     // The bit we are printing now
19     short int bit = (1<<15);
20
21     int count;                   // Loop counter
22
23     for (count = 0; count < 16; ++count)
24     {
25         if ((bit & value) != 0)
26             std::cout << "X";
27         else
28             std::cout << '-';
29         bit >>= 1;
30     }
31     std::cout << std::endl;
32 }
33 int main()
34 {
35     bit_out(0x55AF);
36     return (0);
37 }
```

(Next Hint 180. Answer 19.)

Program 43: Baseless

We know that 2 is an int. So why does C++ think it's a float and call the wrong function?

```
 1 /**********************************************
 2 * demonstrate the use of derived classes.     *
 3 **********************************************/
 4 #include <iostream>
 5
 6 /**********************************************
 7 * base -- A sample base class.                 *
 8 *         Prints various values.               *
 9 **********************************************/
10 class base
11 {
12         // Constructor defaults
13         // Destructor defaults
14         // Copy constructor defaults
15         // Assignment operator defaults
16     public:
17         // Print a floating point number
18         void print_it(
19             float value // The value to print
20         )
21         {
22             std::cout <<
23                 "Base (float=" << value << ")\n";
24         }
25         // Print an integer value
26         void print_it(
27             int value    // The value to print
28         )
29         {
30             std::cout <<
31                 "Base (int=" << value << ")\n";
32         }
33 };
34
```

```
35 class der
36 {
37        // Constructor defaults
38        // Destructor defaults
39        // Copy constructor defaults
40        // Assignment operator defaults
41    public:
42        // Print a floating point number
43        void print_it(
44            float value // The value to print
45        )
46        {
47            std::cout <<
48                "Der (float=" << value << ")\n";
49        }
50 };
51
52 int main()
53 {
54    der a_var;  // A class to play with
55
56    // Print a value using der::print_it(float)
57    a_var.print_it(1.0);
58
59    // Print a value using base::print_it(int)
60    a_var.print_it(2);
61    return (0);
62 }
```

(Next Hint 330. Answer 58.)

The original version of the UNIX mt command had a unusual error message that appeared when it couldn't understand a command:

```
mt -f /dev/rst8 funny
mt: Can't grok "funny"
```

For those unfamiliar with Robert Heinlein's *Stranger in a Strange Land*, *grok* is a Martian term for *understand*.

This term did not transfer well to other countries. One German programmer went nuts trying to find "grok" in his English/German dictionary.

Program 44: Ordering Problem

The following code is supposed to find the difference between adjacent elements of an array. Why does it fail to work?

```
1 /*********************************************
2  * diff elements -- Print the differences     *
3  *      between adjacent elements of any array. *
4  *********************************************/
5 #include <iostream>
6
7 // Any array containing pairs of values.
8 // Ends with the sentinel -1
9 static int array[12] =
10 {
11     44, 8,
12     50, 33,
13     50, 32,
14     75, 39,
15     83, 33,
16     -1, -1
17 };
18
19 // Array to hold the differences
20 static int diff[6];
21
22 int main()
23 {
24     int i;      // Index into the array
25
26     // Index into the diff results
27     int diff_index;
28
29     i = 0;
30     diff_index = 0;
31     // Difference adjacent elements of an array
32     while (array[i] != 0)
33     {
34         diff[diff_index++] =
35             array[i++] - array[i++];
36     }
37
```

```
38      // Print the results
39      for (i = 0; i < 6; ++i)
40      {
41          std::cout << "diff[" << i << "]= " <<
42              diff[i] << std::endl;
43      }
44      return (0);
45 }
```

(Next Hint 177. Answer 26.)

Real Computer Scientists admire ADA for its overwhelming aesthetic value, but they find it difficult to actually program in it, as it is much too large to implement. Most computer scientists don't notice this because they are still arguing over what else to add to ADA.

Real Computer Scientists despise the idea of actual hardware. Hardware has limitations; software doesn't. It's a real shame that Turing machines are so poor at I/O.

Real Computer Scientists don't comment their code. The identifiers are so long they can't afford the disk space.

Real Computer Scientists don't program in assembler. They don't write in anything less portable than a number two pencil.

Real Computer Scientists don't write code. They occasionally tinker with "programming systems," but those are so high level that they hardly count (and rarely count accurately; precision is for applications).

Real Computer Scientists only write specs for languages that might run on future hardware. Nobody trusts them to write specs for anything homo sapiens will ever be able to fit on a single planet.

Program 45: Triple Surprise

Are a,b,c in descending order? Does the program agree with you?

```
 1  /***********************************************
 2   * test to see if three variables are in order. *
 3   ***********************************************/
 4  #include <iostream>
 5
 6  int main()
 7  {
 8      int a,b,c;  // Three simple variables
 9
10      a = 7;
11      b = 5;
12      c = 3;
13
14      // Test to see if they are in order
15      if (a > b > c)
16          std::cout << "a,b,c are in order\n";
17      else
18          std::cout << "a,b,c are mixed up\n";
19      return (0);
20  }
```

(Next Hint 312. Answer 80.)

The debugger for all DEC computers is called DDT. In the PDP-10 DDT manual there is footnote as to how this name came about:

Historical footnote: DDT was developed at MIT for the PDP-1 computer in 1961. At that time DDT stood for "DEC Debugging Tape." Since then, the idea of an on-line debugging program has propagated throughout the computer industry. DDT programs are now available for all DEC computers. Since media other than tape are now frequently used, the more descriptive name "Dynamic Debugging Technique" has been adopted, retaining the DDT acronym. Confusion between DDT-10 and another well-known pesticide, dichloro-diphenyl-trichloroethylene ($C_{14} H_9 Cl_5$), should be minimal since each attacks a different, and apparently mutually exclusive, class of bugs.

Program 46: Nothing Goes Wrong

Why does the following program sometimes dump core?

```
 1 /*********************************************
 2  * list -- Test out the command list decoder.  *
 3  *                                              *
 4  * Read a command from the input and check to   *
 5  * see if the command decoder can find it.      *
 6  *********************************************/
 7 #include <iostream>
 8 #include <cstring>
 9
10 static inline void do_open() {
11     std::cout << "do_open called\n";
12 }
13 static inline void do_close() {
14     std::cout << "do_close called\n";
15 }
16 static inline void do_save() {
17     std::cout << "do_save called\n";
18 }
19 static inline void do_quit() {
20     exit(0);
21 }
22 /*
23  * The command as a string and
24  * as a function to execute
25  */
26 struct cmd_info {
27     char *const cmd;
28     void (*funct)();
29 };
30
31 /*
32  * List of all possible commands
33  */
34 static cmd_info cmd_list[] = {
35     {"open", do_open},
36     {"close", do_close},
37     {"save", do_save},
38     {"quit", do_quit},
39     {NULL, NULL}
40 };
```

```
41
42  /*********************************************
43   * do_cmd -- Decode a command an execute it.  *
44   *     If the command is not found, output an  *
45   *     error.                                  *
46   *********************************************/
47  static void do_cmd(
48      const char *const cmd
49  ) {
50      struct cmd_info *cur_cmd;
51
52      cur_cmd = cmd_list;
53
54      while (
55          (std::strcmp(cur_cmd->cmd, cmd) != 0) &&
56          cur_cmd != NULL)
57      {
58          cur_cmd++;
59      }
60      if (cur_cmd == NULL) {
61          std::cout << "Command not found\n";
62      } else {
63          cur_cmd->funct();
64      }
65  }
66
67  /*********************************************
68   * main -- Simple test program.              *
69   *********************************************/
70  int main()
71  {
72      char cmd[100];
73      while (1) {
74          std::cout << "Cmd: ";
75          std::cin.getline(cmd, sizeof(cmd));
76
77          do_cmd(cmd);
78      }
79  }
```

(Next Hint 135. Answer 70.)

Program 47: Microsoft Backwardness

Why does the following program fail to open the file when compiled and run under MS-DOS?

```
 1 /*********************************************
 2  * read config file -- Open a configuration   *
 3  *         file and read in the data.          *
 4  *                                             *
 5  * Designed to work on both UNIX and MS-DOS.   *
 6  *                                             *
 7  * Note: Incomplete program.                   *
 8  *********************************************/
 9 #include <iostream>
10 #include <fstream>
11
12 #ifdef MS_DOS
13
14 // DOS path
15 const char name[] = "\root\new\table";
16
17 #else /* MS_DOS */
18
19 // UNIX path
20 const char name[] = "/root/new/table";
21
22 #endif /* MS_DOS */
23
24
25 int main() {
26     // The file to read
27     std::ifstream in_file(name);
28
29     if (in_file.bad())
30     {
31         std::cerr <<
32             "Error: Could not open " << std::endl;
33         std::cerr << name << std::endl;
34         exit (8);
35     }
36
37     return (0);
38 }
```

(Next Hint 217. Answer 37.)

Program 48: File Follies

The following program works just fine for a while, and then it refuses to recognize files that contain the magic number:

```
 1 /*********************************************
 2  * scan -- Scan a directory tree for files that *
 3  *        begin with a magic number.           *
 4  *********************************************/
 5 #include <iostream>
 6 #include <dirent.h>
 7 #include <fcntl.h>
 8 #include <unistd.h>
 9
10 // Linux executable magic #
11 const long int MAGIC = 0x464c457f;
12
13 /*********************************************
14  * next_file -- find a list of files with      *
15  *        magic numbers that match the given    *
16  *        number.                               *
17  *                                              *
18  * Returns the name of the file or              *
19  *        NULL if no more files.                *
20  *********************************************/
21 char *next_file(
22     DIR  *dir    // Directory we are scanning
23 )
24 {
25     // The current directory entry
26     struct dirent *cur_ent;
27
28     while (1) {
29         cur_ent = readdir(dir);
30         if (cur_ent == NULL)
31             return (NULL);
32
33         // Open the fd for the input file
34         int fd = open(cur_ent->d_name, O_RDONLY);
35         if (fd < 0)
36             continue;    // Can't get the file
37                          // so try again
38
39         int magic;       // The file's magic number
40
```

```
41          // Size of the latest read
42          int read_size =
43              read(fd, &magic, sizeof(magic));
44
45          if (read_size != sizeof(magic))
46              continue;
47
48          if (magic == MAGIC)
49          {
50              close(fd);
51              return (cur_ent->d_name);
52          }
53      }
54 }
55
56 /*********************************************
57  * scan_dir -- Scan a directory for the      *
58  *      files we want.                        *
59  *********************************************/
60 void scan_dir(
61     const char dir_name[] // Directory name to use
62 )
63 {
64     // The directory we are reading
65     DIR *dir_info = opendir(dir_name);
66     if (dir_info == NULL)
67         return;
68
69     chdir(dir_name);
70
71     while (1) {
72         char *name = next_file(dir_info);
73         if (name == NULL)
74             break;
75         std::cout << "Found: " << name << '\n';
76     }
77 }
78
79 int main()
80 {
81     scan_dir(".");
82     return (0);
83 }
```

(Next Hint 226. Answer 60.)

Program 49: It's As Easy As Falling off a Link

Why does the following program sometimes dump core?

```
1 #include <iostream>
2 #include <string>
3 /***********************************************
4 * linked_list -- Class to handle a linked list *
5 *              containing a list of strings.  *
6 *                                              *
7 * Member functions:                            *
8 *     add -- Add an item to the list           *
9 *     is_in -- Check to see if a string is     *
10 *                   in the list.              *
11 ***********************************************/
12 class linked_list {
13     private:
14         /*
15          * Node in the list
16          */
17         struct node {
18             // String in this node
19             std::string data;
20
21             // Pointer to next node
22             struct node *next;
23         };
24         //First item in the list
25         struct node *first;
26     public:
27         // Constructor
28         linked_list(void): first(NULL) {};
29         // Destructor
30         ~linked_list();
31     private:
32         // No copy constructor
33         linked_list(const linked_list &);
34
35         // No assignment operator
36         linked_list& operator = (const linked_list &);
```

```
37    public:
38        // Add an item to the list
39        void add(
40            // Item to add
41            const std::string &what
42        ) {
43            // Create a node to add
44            struct node *new_ptr = new node;
45
46            // Add the node
47            new_ptr->next = first;
48            new_ptr->data = what;
49            first = new_ptr;
50        }
51        bool is_in(const std::string &what);
52 };
53 /*********************************************
54  * is_in -- see if a string is in a          *
55  *       linked list.                        *
56  *                                           *
57  * Returns true if string's on the list,     *
58  *               otherwise false.            *
59  *********************************************/
60 bool linked_list::is_in(
61     // String to check for
62     const std::string &what
63 ) {
64     /* current structure we are looking at */
65     struct node *current_ptr;
66
67     current_ptr = first;
68
69     while (current_ptr != NULL) {
70         if (current_ptr->data == what)
71             return (true);
72
73         current_ptr = current_ptr->next;
74     }
75     return (false);
76 }
77
```

```
78 /**********************************************
79  * linked_list::~linked_list -- Delete the      *
80  *      data in the linked list.                *
81  **********************************************/
82 linked_list::~linked_list(void) {
83     while (first != NULL) {
84         delete first;
85         first = first->next;
86     }
87 }
88
89 int main() {
90     linked_list list;    // A list to play with
91
92     list.add("Sam");
93     list.add("Joe");
94     list.add("Mac");
95
96     if (list.is_in("Harry"))
97         std::cout << "Harry is on the list\n";
98     else
99         std::cout << "Could not find Harry\n";
100    return (0);
101 }
```

(Next Hint 186. Answer 77.)

A cleaning lady discovered a scuff mark on the floor of the machine room and decided to remove it. First she tried wax, then an ammonia-based cleaner, and finally, as a last resort, steel wool. The combination proved deadly. Not for the scuff mark, but for the computers.

The next day, when the computing staff came to work, they found all their machines down. Opening the cabinets, they discovered massive shorts in all the circuit boards.

What had happened? The cleaning lady first applied a coating of wax to the floor. The ammonia vaporized the wax, which was sucked into the computers by the cooling fans. Thus every board was coated with an even layer of sticky wax. That wasn't too bad, but next came the steel wool. The steel fibers were sucked into the machine where they stuck to the wax coating on the inside of the machine.

Program 50: What Is Truth, Anyway?

Computers have turned "The truth will set you free" into "The truth will confuse the heck out of you."

```
1 /**********************************************
2 * test bool_name, a function turn booleans into*
3 *               text.                         *
4 **********************************************/
5 #include <iostream>
6 #include <string>
7
8 /**********************************************
9 * bool_name -- given a boolean value, return   *
10 *               the text version.             *
11 *                                             *
12 * Returns:                                    *
13 *      Strings "true" or "false" depending    *
14 *               on value.                     *
15 **********************************************/
16 static const std::string &bool_name(
17     const bool value    // The value to check
18 )
19 {
20     // The "true" value
21     const std::string true_name("true");
22
23     // The "false" value
24     const std::string false_name("false");
25
26     if (value == true)
27         return (true_name);
28
29     return (false_name);
30 }
31
32 int main() {
33     std::cout << "True  is " <<
34         bool_name(true) << std::endl;
35
36     std::cout << "False is " <<
37         bool_name(false) << std::endl;
38     return (0);
39 }
```

(Next Hint 319. Answer 30.)

Program 51: A Surplus of Pluses

The programmer tried to do the right thing when defining the ++x and x++ operators. What does the following program print and why?

```
 1 /***********************************************
 2 * Demonstrate how to define and use increment  *
 3 * operator.                                     *
 4 ***********************************************/
 5 #include <iostream>
 6
 7 /***********************************************
 8 * num -- Class to hold a single number         *
 9 ***********************************************/
10 class num
11 {
12        // Constructor defaults
13        // Destructor defaults
14        // Copy Constructor defaults
15        // Assignment operator defaults
16    public:
17        // Value stored in the function
18        int value;
19
20        // Increment operator (i++)
21        num operator ++(int)
22        {
23            num copy(*this);  // Copy for return
24
25            value++;
26            return (copy);
27        }
28
29        // Increment operator (++i)
30        num &operator ++(void)
31        {
32            value++;
33            return (*this);
34        }
35 };
36
```

```
37 int main()
38 {
39     num i;        // A value to play with
40
41     i.value = 1;
42     ++++i;
43     std::cout << "i is " << i.value << std::endl;
44
45     i.value = 1;
46     i++++;
47     std::cout << "i is " << i.value << std::endl;
48     return (0);
49 }
```

(Next Hint 246. Answer 87.)

Program 52: The Case of the Disappearing Rectangle

What's the area of our sample?

```
1  /**********************************************
2   * Demonstration of the rectangle class.       *
3   **********************************************/
4  #include <iostream>
5
6  /**********************************************
7   * rectangle -- hold constant information about *
8   *               a rectangle.                   *
9   *                                              *
10  * Members:                                     *
11  *      area -- Area of the rectangle.          *
12  *      width -- width of the rectangle.        *
13  *      height - length of the rectangle.       *
14  **********************************************/
15 class rectangle
16 {
17     public:
18         const int area;   // Rectangle's Area
19         const int width;  // Rectangle's Width
20         const int height; // Rectangle's Height
21
22     public:
23         // Create a rectangle and assign the
24         // initial values
25         rectangle(
26             const int i_width,  // Initial width
27             const int i_height  // Initial height
28         ) : width(i_width),
29             height(i_height),
30             area(width*height)
31         {}
32         // Destructor defaults
33         // Copy constructor defaults
34         // Assignment operator defaults
35 };
36
37 int main()
38 {
39     // Rectangle to play with
40     rectangle sample(10, 5);
41
42     std::cout << "Area of sample is " <<
```

```
43          sample.area << std::endl;
44      return (0);
45 }
```

(Next Hint 210. Answer 93.)

Man Bytes Computer

A system administrator for a major university was responsible for keeping several hundred DEC machines running. He quickly learned how to diagnose broken machines and figure out which board was bad. To get a steady supply of spare parts he had to purchase a service contract. This meant that a DEC service representative was supposed to come down, diagnose the machines, and figure out which board was bad and replace it. In practice, the university staff had strict orders to never let the DEC service representative near the machines.

A typical service would start with the administrator telling DEC which board was bad. The service representative would come down, find the broken board on the administrator's desk, and replace it with a good one. No running diagnostics or other work, that was all done for him.

A few years later, DEC instituted a "Smart Spares" program. The idea was that you had someone trained, on site, who could figure out which board was bad and order a replacement from DEC. Of course this suited the university, because it had been operating that way for years.

The catch was that you had to take a class, at DEC, to learn how to diagnose systems. The system administrator jumped at this opportunity. He needed the vacation. He practically slept through the two days of classes. The third day was devoted to a lab. The instructor had set up three machines. The students were divided into groups and were supposed to spend the morning finding out what was wrong with their machine.

Our hero turned on his machine, looked at the flashing lights for a minute, and then said, "Bad disk card." The instructor was a little surprised." "How do you know that?"

"Lights aren't right."

The administrator moved to the next machine, looked at it, and said, "Bad memory interface card." At the next machine, "Bad processor card."

Three machines down. This exercise was supposed to take three groups all morning, and this one guy had diagnosed all the machines in two minutes flat. (I talked to him a while back, and he told me that if he knew he was being timed, he would have worked faster.)

(continued on page 79)

Program 53: Maximum Confusion

The max function is simple, the test code is simple, and the answer is . . . . Well, you figure it out.

```
1 /*********************************************
2 * test_max -- Test the max function.         *
3 *********************************************/
4 #include <iostream>
5
6 /*********************************************
7 * max -- return the larger of two integers.  *
8 *                                            *
9 * Returns:                                   *
10 *     biggest of the two numbers.            *
11 *********************************************/
12 const int &max(
13     const int &i1,      // A number
14     const int &i2       // Another number
15 )
16 {
17     if (i1 > i2)
18         return (i1);
19     return (i2);
20 }
21
22 int main()
23 {
24     // I is the biggest of the two expression
25     const int &i = max(1+2, 3+4);
26
27     std::cout <<
28         "The biggest expression is " <<
29         i << std::endl;
30
31     return (0);
32 }
```

(Next Hint 289. Answer 22.)

To err is human. To really fowl up you need a computer.

Program 54: Jumping off the Deep End

Why does this program leak memory?

```
 1 /*********************************************
 2  * Combine strings with a variable length    *
 3  *       string class.                        *
 4  *********************************************/
 5 #include <setjmp.h>
 6 #include <iostream>
 7 #include <cstring>
 8
 9 // Place to store jump information
10 static jmp_buf top_level;
11
12 // Longest string combination allowed.
13 static const unsigned int MAX_LENGTH = 30;
14
15 /*********************************************
16  * combine -- Combine two strings with        *
17  *       limit checking                        *
18  *********************************************/
19 static std::string combine(
20     const std::string &first,   // First string
21     const std::string &second   // Second string
22 )
23 {
24     // Strings put together
25     std::string together = first + second;
26
27     if (together.length() > MAX_LENGTH) {
28         longjmp(top_level, 5);
29     }
30     return (together);
31 }
32
33 int main()
34 {
35     std::string first("First ");
36     int i;
37
```

```
38    for (i = 0; i < 10; i++) {
39
40        // Save our place
41        if (setjmp(top_level) == 0)
42        {
43            first = combine(first,
44                    std::string("second "));
45        } else {
46            std::cout <<
47                "Length limit exceeded\n";
48            break;
49        }
50    }
51    return (0);
52 }
```

(Next Hint 146. Answer 66.)

Man Bytes Computer *(continued from page 76)*

Undaunted, the instructor moved over to the machine reserved for the afternoon problem. This one has been set up by field service and was supposed to have a really tough problem, next to impossible to find.

The instructor knew the problem couldn't be identified by looking at the lights and waited to see what our hero would do. The guy opened the back, and even before he hit the "On" switch pointed to a board and said "That board is bad; chip U18. It'll cause an intermittent data bus parity error."

Now the instructor knew that the guy was good, but spotting a bad board without even turning the machine on? Impossible.

"How do you know it's bad?" he asked.

The administrator pointed to a small blue label in the corner. "See that dot? I put it there so I'd be sure that DEC didn't trade me back my own boards. This board is from the university. I'm the one who originally found the problem and showed it to DEC field service."

The morning and afternoon's problems now solved in the space of about 10 minutes, the class decided it was time to go out for pizza and beer.

Program 55: Sheepish Programming

Farmer Brown, a sheep farmer, had a neighbor who could just look at a flock and tell how many sheep there were at a glance. He wondered how his friend could count so fast, so he asked him.

"Ian, how can you tell how many sheep you have so quickly?"

"Simple," Ian replied. "I just count the legs and divide by 4."

Farmer Brown was so impressed by this that he wrote a short C++ program to verify the Ian sheep-counting algorithm. It wouldn't work for large herds. Why?

```
1 /***********************************************
2  * sheep -- Count sheep by counting the        *
3  *          number of legs and dividing by 4.  *
4  ***********************************************/
5 #include <iostream>
6
7 /*
8  * The number of legs in some different
9  * size herds.
10  */
11 const short int small_herd  =   100;
12 const short int medium_herd =  1000;
13 const short int large_herd  = 10000;
14
15 /***********************************************
16  * report_sheep -- Given the number of legs,   *
17  *      tell us how many sheep we have.         *
18  ***********************************************/
19 static void report_sheep(
20     const short int legs       // Number of legs
21 )
22 {
23     std::cout <<
24         "The number of sheep is: " <<
25                 (legs/4) << std::endl;
26 }
27
28 int main() {
29     report_sheep(small_herd*4); // Expect 100
30     report_sheep(medium_herd*4);// Expect 1000
31     report_sheep(large_herd*4); // Expect 10000
32     return (0);
33 }
```

(Next Hint 165. Answer 1.)

Program 56: The Magic Is Gone from the Program

The following program is designed to see if two files in two directories contain a magic number.

In our test case, we have the files:

    first/first

    second/second

Both these files contain the magic number.

What does the program output and why?

```
 1 /***********************************************
 2  * scan_dir -- Scan directories for magic files *
 3  *       and report the results.                *
 4  *                                              *
 5  * Test on the directories "first" and "second".*
 6  ***********************************************/
 7 #include <iostream>
 8 #include <dirent.h>
 9 #include <fcntl.h>
10 #include <unistd.h>
11 const long int MAGIC = 0x464c457f; // Linux executable magic #
12 /***********************************************
13  * next_file -- find a list of files with magic *
14  *       numbers that match the given number.   *
15  *                                              *
16  * Returns the name of the file or              *
17  *       NULL if no more files.                 *
18  ***********************************************/
19 char *next_file(
20     DIR  *dir             // Directory to scan
21 ) {
22     // Current entry in the dir
23     struct dirent *cur_ent;
24
25     while (1) {
26
27         cur_ent = readdir(dir);
28         if (cur_ent == NULL)
29             return (NULL);
30
31         int fd = open(cur_ent->d_name, O_RDONLY);
32         if (fd < 0) {
33             // Can't get the file so try again
34             continue;
35         }
```

```
36
37        int magic;        // The file's magic number
38
39        // Size of the header read
40        int read_size =
41            read(fd, &magic, sizeof(magic));
42
43        if (read_size != sizeof(magic)) {
44            close(fd);
45            continue;
46        }
47
48        if (magic == MAGIC) {
49            close(fd);
50            return (cur_ent->d_name);
51        }
52        close(fd);
53    }
54 }
55 /*********************************************
56  * scan_dir -- Scan a directory for the files   *
57  *      we want.                                 *
58  *********************************************/
59 char *scan_dir(
60     const char dir_name[] // Directory name to use
61 ) {
62     // Directory to scan
63     DIR *dir_info = opendir(dir_name);
64     if (dir_info == NULL)
65         return (NULL);
66
67     chdir(dir_name);
68
69     // Name of the file we just found
70     char *name = next_file(dir_info);
71     closedir(dir_info);
72
73     chdir("..");           // Undo the original chdir
74
75     return (name);
76 }
77
```

```
78 int main() {
79     // Find a file in the directory "first"
80     char *first_ptr = scan_dir("first");
81
82     // Find a file in the directory "second"
83     char *second_ptr = scan_dir("second");
84
85     // Print the information about the dir first
86     if (first_ptr == NULL) {
87         std::cout << "First: NULL ";
88     } else {
89         std::cout << "First: " << first_ptr << " ";
90     }
91     std::cout << '\n';
92
93     // Print the information about the dir second
94     if (second_ptr == NULL) {
95         std::cout << "Second: NULL ";
96     } else {
97         std::cout << "Second: " << second_ptr << " ";
98     }
99     std::cout << '\n';
100    return (0);
101 }
```

(Next Hint 86. Answer 100.)

Real Software Engineers work from 9 to 5, because that is the way the job is described in the formal spec. Working late would feel like using an undocumented external procedure.

Program 57: How Not to Read a File

What kind of portability problems exist in the following code?

```
1 #include <iostream>
2
3 /*
4  * A data structure consisting of a flag
5  * which indicates which long int parameter
6  * follows.
7  */
8 struct data
9 {
10     // Flag indicating what's to follow
11     char flag;
12
13     // Value of the parameter
14     long int value;
15 };
16
17 /*********************************************
18  * read_data -- Read data from the given file   *
19  *********************************************/
20 void read_data(
21     std::istream &in_file,      // File to read
22     struct data &what       // Data to get
23 )
24 {
25     in_file.read(
26         dynamic_cast<char *>(&what),
27         sizeof(what));
28 }
```

(Next Hint 161. Answer 71.)

One electronic time card program had an interesting way of finishing up:

```
Timecard entry complete
Press 'Enter' to exit the program.
```

Program 58: Weird Names

The subroutine tmp_name is designed to return the name of a temporary file. The idea is to generate a unique name each time it is called: /var/tmp/tmp.0, /var/tmp/tmp.1, /var/tmp/tmp.2, . . .

The names that are generated are certainly unique, but not what the programmer intended.

```
1 /**********************************************
2  * tmp_test -- test out the tmp_name function.  *
3  **********************************************/
4 #include <iostream>
5 #include <cstdio>
6 #include <cstring>
7 #include <sys/param.h>
8 /**********************************************
9  * tmp_name -- return a temporary file name    *
10 *                                             *
11 * Each time this function is called, a new    *
12 *       name will be returned.                *
13 *                                             *
14 * Returns: Pointer to the new file name.      *
15 **********************************************/
16 char *tmp_name(void) {
17     // The name we are generating
18     char name[MAXPATHLEN];
19
20     // The base of the generated name
21     const char DIR[] = "/var/tmp/tmp";
22
23     // Sequence number for last digit
24     static int sequence = 0;
25
26     ++sequence; /* Move to the next file name */
27
28     sprintf(name, "%s.%d", DIR, sequence);
29     return(name);
30 }
31 int main() {
32     char *a_name = tmp_name();  // A tmp name
33     std::cout << "Name: " << a_name << std::endl;
34     return(0);
35 }
```

(Next Hint 176. Answer 18.)

Program 59: Son of Weird Names

This program is designed to generate unique names every time tmp_name is called. To test it, we decided to print a couple of names. Yet our test isn't working. Why?

```
1  /*********************************************
2   * test the tmp_name function.              *
3   *********************************************/
4  #include <iostream>
5  #include <cstdio>
6  #include <cstring>
7  #include <sys/param.h>
8  /*********************************************
9   * tmp_name -- return a temporary file name. *
10  *                                           *
11  * Each time this function is called, a new  *
12  *       name will be returned.              *
13  *                                           *
14  * Returns                                   *
15  *       Pointer to the new file name.       *
16  *********************************************/
17 char *tmp_name(void)
18 {
19     // The name we are generating
20     static char name[MAXPATHLEN];
21
22     // The directory to put the temporary file in
23     const char DIR[] = "/var/tmp/tmp";
24
25     // Sequence number for last digit
26     static int sequence = 0;
27
28     ++sequence; /* Move to the next file name */
29
30     std::sprintf(name, "%s.%d", DIR, sequence);
31     return(name);
32 }
33
```

```
34 int main()
35 {
36     // The first temporary name
37     char *a_name = tmp_name();
38
39     // The second temporary name
40     char *b_name = tmp_name();
41
42     std::cout << "Name (a): " << a_name << endl;
43     std::cout << "Name (b): " << b_name << endl;
44     return(0);
45 }
```

(Next Hint 322. Answer 64.)

I was assigned to program a newly built light panel. Light #1 was supposed to be "Data Fail," light #2 "Change Filter," light #3 "Oil Pressure Low" and so on.

A short test revealed that the panel was wired wrong. Light #1 was "Oil Pressure Low," Light #2 "Oil Pressure Low," and so on.

I carefully copied down the numbers for the lights and then hunted up the hardware designer.

"Woody," I said, "the lights are wired up wrong."

"Do you know how they are wired up now?"

I handed him my list. He took it from my hands, looked it over quickly, walked over to the copier and made a copy. Then he gave me a copy (not even the original) and said, "Here's the new specification."

Program 60: Grandson of Weird Names

So we've fixed our program again and now are using C++ strings. But things still don't work right. Why?

```cpp
1 #include <iostream>
2 #include <string>
3
4 /***********************************************
5  * tmp_name -- return a temporary file name    *
6  *                                             *
7  * Each time this function is called, a new    *
8  * name will be returned.                      *
9  *                                             *
10 * Returns                                     *
11 *       String containing the name.           *
12 ***********************************************/
13 std::string &tmp_name()
14 {
15     // The name we are generating
16     std::string name;
17
18     // Sequence number for last digit
19     static int sequence = 0;
20
21     ++sequence; // Move to the next file name
22
23     name = "tmp";
24
25     // Put in the squence digit
26     name += static_cast<char>(sequence + '0');
27
28     return(name);
29 }
30
31 int main()
32 {
33     std::string name1 = tmp_name();
34
35     std::cout <<"Name1: " << name1 << '\n';
36     return(0);
37 }
```

(Next Hint 361. Answer 36.)

Program 61: Looking Through a Dictionary Slowly

I wrote the following program when I was a junior at Caltech. (It was written in Pascal originally.) I was a poor speller, so I needed something to help me find words in the dictionary.

I decided to write a program to read the dictionary into a binary tree (a data structure I just learned about) and to look for words in it.

Binary trees are supposed to be efficient data structures, but this program takes an awfully long time to execute.

Why?

```
1  /**********************************************
2   * find_word -- find a word in the dictionary. *
3   *                                              *
4   * Usage:                                       *
5   *      find_word <word-start> [<word-start>...] *
6   **********************************************/
7  #include <iostream>
8  #include <fstream>
9  #include <iomanip>
10 #include <cctype>
11 #include <cstring>
12 #include <cstdlib>
13
14 /**********************************************
15  * tree -- A simple binary tree class         *
16  *                                            *
17  * Member functions:                          *
18  *      enter -- Add an entry to the tree      *
19  *      find -- See if an entry is in the tree. *
20  **********************************************/
21 class tree
22 {
23     private:
24         // The basic node of a tree
25         class node {
26             private:
27                 // tree to the right
28                 node    *right;
29
30                 // tree to the left
31                 node    *left;
32             public:
33                 // data for this tree
34                 char    *data;
```

```
35
36          public:
37              node() :
38                  right(NULL), left(NULL),
39                  data(NULL) {}
40              // Destructor defaults
41          private:
42              // No copy constructor
43              node(const node &);
44
45              // No assignment operator
46              node & operator = (const node &);
47
48              // Let tree manipulate our data
49              friend class tree;
50
51          };
52
53      // the top of the tree
54      node *root;
55
56      // Enter a new node into a tree or
57      // sub-tree
58      void enter_one(
59          // Node of sub-tree to look at
60          node *&node,
61
62          // Word to add
63          const char *const data
64      );
65
66      // Find an item in the tree
67      void find_one(
68          // Prefix to search for
69          const char start[],
70
71          // Node to start search
72          const node *const node,
73
74          // Keep looking flag
75          const bool look
76      );
77  public:
78      tree(void) { root = NULL;}
79      // Destructor defaults
80  private:
81      // No copy constructor
```

```
82          tree(const tree &);
83
84          // No assignment operator
85          tree & operator = (const tree &);
86
87      public:
88          // Add a new data to our tree
89          void enter(
90              // Data to add
91              const char *const data
92          ) {
93              enter_one(root, data);
94          }
95
96          // Find all words that start
97          // with the given prefix
98          void find(
99              const char start[]  // Starting string
100         )
101         {
102             find_one(start, root, true);
103         }
104 };
105
106 /*********************************************
107  * tree::enter_one -- enter a data into      *
108  *      the tree                             *
109  *********************************************/
110 void tree::enter_one(
111     node *&new_node,        // Sub-tree to look at
112     const char *const data // Word to add
113 )
114 {
115     int  result;         // result of strcmp
116
117     // see if we have reached the end
118     if (new_node == NULL) {
119         new_node = new node;
120
121         new_node->left = NULL;
122         new_node->right = NULL;
123         new_node->data = strdup(data);
124     }
125
126     result = strcmp(new_node->data, data);
127     if (result == 0) {
128         return;
```

```
129        }
130
131        if (result < 0)
132            enter_one(new_node->right, data);
133        else
134            enter_one(new_node->left, data);
135 }
136
137 /*********************************************
138  * tree::find_one -- find words that match this *
139  *                      one in the tree.         *
140  *********************************************/
141 void tree::find_one(
142        const char start[],   // Start of the work
143        const node *const top,// Top node
144        const bool look        // Keep looking
145 )
146 {
147     if (top == NULL)
148         return;                    // short tree
149
150     // Result of checking our prefix
151     // against the word
152     int cmp = strncmp(start,
153             top->data, strlen(start));
154
155     if ((cmp < 0) && (look))
156         find_one(start, top->left, true);
157     else if ((cmp > 0) && (look))
158         find_one(start, top->right, true);
159
160     if (cmp != 0)
161         return;
162
163     /*
164      * We found a string that starts this one.
165      * Keep searching and print things.
166      */
167     find_one(start, top->left, false);
168     std::cout << top->data << '\n';
169     find_one(start, top->right, false);
170 }
171
172 int main(int argc, char *argv[])
173 {
174     // A tree to hold a set of words
175     tree dict_tree;
```

```
176
177     // The dictionary to search
178     std::ifstream dict_file("/usr/dict/words");
179
180     if (dict_file.bad()) {
181         std::cerr <<
182             "Error: Unable to open "
183             "dictionary file\n";
184         exit (8);
185     }
186
187     /*
188      * Read the dictionary and construct the tree
189      */
190     while (1) {
191         char line[100]; // Line from the file
192
193         dict_file.getline(line, sizeof(line));
194
195         if (dict_file.eof())
196             break;
197
198         dict_tree.enter(strdup(line));
199     }
200     /*
201      * Search for each word
202      */
203     while (argc > 1) {
204         std::cout << "------ " << argv[1] << '\n';
205         dict_tree.find(argv[1]);
206         ++argv;
207         --argc;
208     }
209     return (0);
210 }
```

(Next Hint 42. Answer 74.)

Program 62: Zipping Along

What could be simpler than assigning a value to two constants and printing them out? Yet in something so simple there is a problem. Why is one of the zip codes wrong?

```
1 /***********************************************
2  * print_zip -- Print out a couple of zip codes.*
3  ***********************************************/
4 #include <iostream>
5 #include <iomanip>
6
7 int main()
8 {
9     // Zip code for San Diego
10    const long int san_diego_zip = 92126;
11
12    // Zip code for Boston
13    const long int boston_zip    = 02126;
14
15    std::cout << "San Diego " << std::setw(5) <<
16        std::setfill('0') <<
17        san_diego_zip << std::endl;
18
19    std::cout << "Boston    " << std::setw(5) <<
20        std::setfill('0') <<
21        boston_zip << std::endl;
22
23    return (0);
24 }
```

(Next Hint 206. Answer 15.)

Oualline's Law of Computers

1. There is nothing so important in computer science as a firm grasp of the obvious.

2. There is nothing obvious about computers.

5

C CODE, C CODE BREAK

In spite of the efforts of language designers, there is still a lot of C code out there. C is its own language and has its own set of problems. Here are a few unique and special mistakes that only a C programmer can make.

Program 63: Name Game

This program is supposed to combine your first and last names and print them. A sample run should look like:

```
First: John
Last:  Smith
Hello: John Smith
Thank you for using Acme Software.
```

But what does the program really do?

```c
 1 /*********************************************
 2  * Greetings -- Ask the user for his first    *
 3  *       name and his last name.              *
 4  *       Then issue a greeting.               *
 5  *********************************************/
 6 #include <stdio.h>
 7 #include <string.h>
 8 int main()
 9 {
10     char first[100];    /* The first name */
11     char last[100];     /* The last name */
12     char full_name[201];/* The full name */
13
14     /* Get the first name */
15     printf("First: ");
16     fgets(first, sizeof(first), stdin);
17
18     /* Get the last name */
19     printf("Last:  ");
20     fgets(last, sizeof(last), stdin);
21
22     /* Make    full_name = "<first> <last>" */
23     strcpy(full_name, first);
24     strcat(full_name, " ");
25     strcat(full_name, last);
26
27     /* Greet the user by name */
28     printf("Hello %s\n", full_name);
29     printf("Thank you for "
30             "using Acme Software.\n");
31     return (0);
32 }
```

(Next Hint 340. Answer 33.)

Program 64: π in Your Eye

The file *math.h* defines the constant M_PI. What do we get when we print this constant?

```
 1 /*********************************************
 2  * PI -- Test program to see verify that      *
 3  *       the value  of "pi" in math.h is       *
 4  *       correct.                              *
 5  *********************************************/
 6 /* math.h defines M_PI */
 7 #include <math.h>
 8 #include <stdio.h>
 9
10 int main()
11 {
12     printf("pi is %d\n", M_PI);
13     return (0);
14 }
```

(Next Hint 198. Answer 10.)

Someone at Caltech wrote a program to give you a nice greeting when you signed on. This was a very smart program; part of the logic looked at the author's account to see if a new version of the program had been released. If it had, the program replaced itself with the later version.

One day the author graduated and his account was deleted. The program detected this as an error condition and promptly issued a message:

?LGNPFB Program fall down and go boom.

Program 65: Temporary Insanity

Sometimes a bogus file name is returned. Sometimes the program dumps core. Why?

```
 1 /*********************************************
 2  * full_test -- Test the full_name function    *
 3  *********************************************/
 4 #define PATH "/usr/tmp"
 5
 6 /*********************************************
 7  * full_name -- Given the name of a file,      *
 8  *       return a full path name.              *
 9  *                                             *
10  * Returns: Absolute path to the file name.    *
11  *********************************************/
12 char *full_name(
13     const char name[]    /* Base file name */
14 )
15 {
16     /* Full file name */
17     static char file_name[100];
18
19     strcpy(file_name, PATH);
20     strcat(file_name, '/');
21     strcat(file_name, name);
22     return (file_name);
23 }
24
25 int main()
26 {
27     /* Test the full_name funtion */
28     printf("Full name is %s\n",
29             full_name("data"));
30     return (0);
31 }
32
```

(Next Hint 320. Answer 41.)

Program 66: Buffer to Nowhere

The programmer decided to speed up the buffered I/O by increasing the size of the buffer. Normally this would make things faster, but in this case it makes things strange. Why?

```
1  /**********************************************
2   * buffer demo.  Show how big buffers can speed *
3   * up I/O.                                      *
4   **********************************************/
5  #include <stdio.h>
6
7  /* Nice big buffer */
8  #define BUF_SIZE   (50 * 1024)
9
10 /**********************************************
11  * print_stuff -- Print a bunch of stuff in a  *
12  *       big buffer.                           *
13  **********************************************/
14 void print_stuff(void)
15 {
16     // Buffer to hold the data
17     char buffer[BUF_SIZE];
18
19     // Printing counter.
20     int i;
21
22     /* Things go much faster with this */
23     setbuf(stdout, buffer);
24
25     for (i = 0; i < 10; ++i)
26         printf("Hello world\n");
27 }
28
29
30 int main()
31 {
32     print_stuff();
33     printf("That's all\n");
34     return (0);
35 }
```

(Next Hint 74. Answer 83.)

Program 67: Let's Play "Hide the Problem"

The following program dumps core with a floating-point divide error on UNIX. This is puzzling because we do no floating-point operations.

In order to find the problem, we've put in a few `printf` statements and discovered that it's happening somewhere before the function call. We can tell this because we never see the "starting" message.

```
1  /**********************************************
2   * Compute a simple average.  Because this    *
3   * takes a long time (?) we output some        *
4   * chatter as we progress through the system.  *
5   **********************************************/
6  #include <stdio.h>
7
8  /**********************************************
9   * average -- Compute the average given the   *
10  *        total of the series and the number   *
11  *        of items in the series.              *
12  *                                             *
13  * Returns:                                     *
14  *        The average.                          *
15  **********************************************/
16 int average(
17     const int total,// The total of the series
18     const int count // The number of items
19 )
20 {
21     return (total/count);
22 }
23
24 int main()
25 {
26     int ave;     // Average of the number
27
28     printf("Starting....");
29     ave = average(32, 0);
30     printf("..done\n");
31
32     printf("The answer is %d\n", ave);
33     return (0);
34 }
```

(Next Hint 108. Answer 68.)

Program 68: Miscalculating

The assignment here is to make a four-function calculator. The user is supposed to type in an operator and a number, and the calculator goes to work. For example:

```
Enter operator and value: + 10
Total: 10
```

But things don't go as expected.

```c
1  /**********************************************
2   * calc -- Simple 4 function calculator.      *
3   *                                            *
4   * Usage:                                     *
5   *      $ calc                                *
6   *      Enter operator and value: + 5         *
7   *                                            *
8   * At the end of each operation the accumulated *
9   * results are printed.                       *
10  **********************************************/
11 #include <stdio.h>
12 int main() {
13     char oper;  /* Operator for our calculator */
14     int  result;/* Current result */
15     int value;  /* Value for the operation */
16
17     result = 0;
18     while (1)
19     {
20         char line[100]; // Line from the user
21         printf("Enter operator and value:");
22
23         fgets(line, sizeof(line), stdin);
24         sscanf(line, "%c %d", oper, value);
25
26         switch (oper) {
27             case '+':
28                 result += value; break;
29             case '-':
30                 result -= value; break;
31             case '*':
32                 result *= value; break;
```

```
33              case '/':
34                  if (value == 0)
35                      printf("Divide by 0 error\n");
36                  else
37                      result /= value;
38                  break;
39              case 'q':
40                  exit (0);
41              default:
42                  printf("Bad operator entered\n"); break;
43          }
44      printf("Total: %d\n", result);
45      }
46 }
```

(Next Hint 73. Answer 95.)

━━━━━━━━━━━━━━━━━━━━

One company had a problem. Some of its customers were deleting the company name and copyright from its software. The programmers were asked to come up with a way to prevent this. So they put in some code to checksum the copyright, and if it came out wrong, they would issue an error message:

```
Fatal error:
        Water buffalos need immediate feeding
Call 1-800-555-1234 for technical support.
```

The idea was that this error message would be so strange that the miscreant would call technical support to find out what it meant. (What it really meant was, "I modified your program illegally.")

━━━━━━━━━━━━━━━━━━━━

Program 69: Sum Problem

This program is designed to add three numbers, 1, 2, and 3. But when we run it, the program produces the result:

```
Sum is 1343432864
```

Why?

```
1  /*********************************************
2   * sum_test -- Test the sum function         *
3   *********************************************/
4  #include <stdio.h>
5
6  /*********************************************
7   * sum -- Sum up three numbers               *
8   *                                           *
9   * Returns: The sum of the numbers.          *
10  *********************************************/
11 int sum(i1, i2, i3)
12 {
13    int i1;       /* The first number */
14    int i2;       /* The second number */
15    int i3;       /* The third number */
16
17    return (i1 + i2 + i3);
18 }
19
20 int main()
21 {
22    printf("Sum is %d\n", sum(1, 2, 3));
23    return (0);
24 }
25
```

(Next Hint 69. Answer 94.)

"Yacc" owes much to a most stimulating collection of users, who have goaded me beyond my inclination and frequently beyond my ability in their endless search for "one more feature." Their irritating unwillingness to learn how to do things my way has usually led to my doing things their way; most of the time, they have been right.

— S. C. Johnson, "Yacc guide acknowledgments"

Program 70: Two Simple

Why does 2 + 2 = 5986?

```
 1 /*********************************************
 2  * two_plus_two -- So what is 2+2 anyway?      *
 3  *********************************************/
 4 #include <stdio.h>
 5
 6 int main()
 7 {
 8     /* Result of the addition */
 9     int answer = 2 + 2;
10
11     printf("The answer is %d\n");
12     return (0);
13 }
```

(Next Hint 164. Answer 85.)

At the bottom of your bank checks is a series of numbers that indicates your bank and account number. A crook opened an account in New York with $5. He then created his own checks. They where the same as his real checks except that the bank number was modified so that it referred to a bank in Los Angeles.

Next he opened another account in New York and used a $10,000 check for the initial deposit. The check went into the automatic sorting equipment, and the computer saw the bank number for Los Angeles and sent the check to L.A. The bank in L.A. saw that this check wasn't for it, so it sent the check back to the clearing house in New York. It went back in the automatic sorting equipment, the computer saw the L.A. bank number, and it's sent back to L.A.

The check was now in an endless cycle going back and forth between New York and L.A. While it circled round and round, the crook went to the bank where he deposited first the check and asked for all his money. The clerk looked up the last deposit, saw that it was two weeks ago, and assumed that the check had cleared. After all, it takes only a couple of days for a New York check to get to the proper bank. So the clerk gave the crook $10,000, and he disappeared.

Several weeks later, the check got so beat up that it could no longer be dumped in the automatic sorting equipment. So it was hand sorted and finally given to the right bank.

(This is called "cashing in on the float" in a big way.)

Program 71: Unsynchronized

The assignment here is to make a four-function calculator. The user is supposed to type in an operator and a number, and the calculator goes to work. For example:

```
Enter operator and value: + 10
Total: 10
```

But things don't go as expected.

```
1  /***********************************************
2  * calc -- Simple 4 function calculator.       *
3  *                                             *
4  * Usage:                                      *
5  *        $ calc                               *
6  *        Enter operator and value: + 5        *
7  *                                             *
8  * At the end of each operation the acculated  *
9  * results are printed.                        *
10 ***********************************************/
11 #include <stdio.h>
12 #include <stdlib.h>
13 int main() {
14     char oper;  /* Operator for our calculator */
15     int  result;/* Current result */
16     int value;  /* Value for the operation */
17
18     result = 0;
19     while (1)
20     {
21         printf("Enter operator and value:");
22         scanf("%c %d", &oper, &value);
23
24         switch (oper) {
25             case '+':
26                 result += value;
27                 break;
28             case '-':
29                 result -= value;
30                 break;
31             case '*':
32                 result *= value;
33                 break;
```

```
34              case '/':
35                  if (value == 0)
36                      printf("Divide by 0 error\n");
37                  else
38                      result /= value;
39                  break;
40              case 'q':
41                  exit (0);
42              default:
43                  printf("Bad operator entered\n"); break;
44          }
45          printf("Total: %d\n", result);
46      }
47 }
```

(Next Hint 224. Answer 28.)

Real Programmers disdain structured programming. Structured programming is for compulsive neurotics who were prematurely toilet-trained. Those people wear neckties and carefully line up pencils on otherwise clear desks.

Real Programmers don't bring brown-bag lunches. If the vending machine doesn't sell it, they don't eat it. Vending machines don't sell quiche.

Program 72: No End in Sight

This simple program is to copy the standard input to the standard output. It's one of the first I/O-related programs that a student writes.

```
1 /*********************************************
2  * copy -- Copy stdin to stdout.            *
3  *********************************************/
4 #include <stdio.h>
5
6 int main()
7 {
8      // Character to copy
9      char ch;
10
11     while ((ch = getchar()) != EOF)
12     {
13         putchar(ch);
14     }
15     return (0);
16 }
```

(Next Hint 15. Answer 63.)

"There are two ways of constructing a software design. One way is to make it so simple that there are obviously no deficiencies, and the other way is to make it so complicated that there are no obvious deficiencies."
— C. A. R. Hoare

This page intentionally left blank. Except that we put this paragraph on it, so it's not blank anymore.

6

PREMATURE BREAKAGE

The C++ preprocessor gives you a lot more flexibility with the language. It also gives you a lot of new ways of screwing up.

Program 73: Pointless

What are the variable types of sam and joe?

```
 1 /**********************************************
 2  * Toy program that declares two variables     *
 3  **********************************************/
 4 #define CHAR_PTR char *
 5
 6 int main()
 7 {
 8     CHAR_PTR sam, joe;
 9
10     return (0);
11 }
```

(Next Hint 298. Answer 78.)

I worked on the first commercial waterjet cutter. The machine was essentially a giant squirt gun that cut out tennis shoe insoles with a high pressure jet of water.

Since it was the first one ever made, we spent a lot of time tuning it. About a year. We had a deal with the tennis shoe maker who was buying it. They would give us free raw material to test with if we sent the cut pieces back to them.

For about a year we tested. Since we wanted to get consistent results we almost always used the same test size: 9 right. We dutifully boxed up the cut pieces and sent them to the tennis shoe maker so that they could make shoes out of them. Or so we thought.

About a week before we were scheduled to ship the machine we got a call from someone at the tennis shoe plant.

Tennis shoe plant: "Are you the people who keep sending all the 9 rights to us?"

Us: "Yes."

Plant: "Finally, I found you people. I've been trying to track you down for a year. Purchasing has no record of any cut piece order for you and it was very difficult to find you."

Us: "Is there a problem?"

Plant: "Yes. Do you realize that you've shipped us 10,000 nine rights and no lefts?"

Program 74: Gross Error

Why does the following program report a syntax error on line 16. What's wrong with line 16?

```
1 /**********************************************
2  * gross -- Print out a table of 1 to 10 gross. *
3  **********************************************/
4 // A Gross is a dozen - dozen
5 #define GROSS (12 ** 2)
6
7 #include <iostream>
8
9 int main()
10 {
11     int i;        // Index into the table
12
13     for (i = 1; i <= 10; ++i)
14     {
15         std::cout << i << " gross is " <<
16             (GROSS * i) << '\n';
17     }
18
19     return (0);
20 }
```

(Next Hint 275. Answer 79.)

There are two ways to write error-free programs.
Only the third one works.

Program 75: Quick Exit

The ABORT macro is designed to issue an error message and exit. The program should abort when something goes wrong.

The program does exit when we have an error. It also exits when we don't have an error. In fact, it exits no matter what.

Why?

```
 1 /*********************************************
 2  * Test the square_root function.            *
 3  *********************************************/
 4 #include <iostream>
 5 #include <math.h>
 6
 7 /*********************************************
 8  * ABORT -- print an error message and abort. *
 9  *********************************************/
10 #define ABORT(msg) \
11     std::cerr << msg << std::endl;exit(8);
12 /*********************************************
13  * square_root -- Find the square root of the *
14  *       value.                               *
15  *                                            *
16  * Returns:                                   *
17  *       The square root.                     *
18  *********************************************/
19 static int square_root(
20     const int value
22 ) {
23     if (value < 0)
24         ABORT("Illegal square root");
25
26     return (int(sqrt(float(value))));
27 }
28
29 int main() {
30     int square; // A number that's square
31     int root;   // The square root of the number
32
33     square = 5 * 5;
34     root = square_root(square);
35
36     std::cout << "Answer is: " << root << '\n';
37     return (0);
38 }
```

(Next Hint 33. Answer 105.)

Program 76: Double Trouble

The macro DOUBLE is designed to double the value of its argument. The test program prints out the DOUBLE values of the numbers for 1 through 5. Yet something goes wrong. What's happening?

```
1  /*********************************************
2   * Double -- Print double table.             *
3   *                                           *
4   * Print the numbers 1 through 5 and their   *
5   *      doubles.                             *
6   *********************************************/
7  #include <iostream>
8
9  /*********************************************
10  * DOUBLE -- Given a number return its double. *
11  *********************************************/
12 #define DOUBLE(x) (x * 2)
13
14 int main()
15 {
16     int i;       // Number to print and to double
17
18     for (i = 0; i < 5; ++i) {
19         std::cout << "The double of " << i+1 <<
20             " is " << DOUBLE(i+1) << std::endl;
21     }
22
23     return (0);
24 }
```

(Next Hint 133. Answer 46.)

"The C programming language — a language that combines the flexibility of assembly language with the power of assembly language."

Program 77: No Value

The following program fails to compile because the value is undefined. We never use the variable value, so what's the problem?

```
1  /**********************************************
2   * double -- Print a double table for the      *
3   *          numbers 1 through 10.              *
4   **********************************************/
5  #include <iostream>
6
7  /**********************************************
8   * DOUBLE -- Macro to double the value of a    *
9   *            number.                          *
10  **********************************************/
11 #define DOUBLE (value) ((value) + (value))
12
13 int main()
14 {
15     // Counter for the double list
16     int counter;
17
18     for (counter = 1; counter <= 10; ++counter)
19     {
20         std::cout << "Twice " << counter << " is " <<
21             DOUBLE(counter) << '\n';
22     }
23
24     return (0);
25 }
```

(Next Hint 118. Answer 113.)

Program 78: Margin of Error

If we have a paper width of 8.5 inches and use 1 inch for margins (1/2 inch each side), how much usable space do we have left? Anyone can see that the result is 7.5 inches. But this program sees things differently. What's happening?

```
 1 /**********************************************
 2  * paper_size -- Find the usable width on      *
 3  *      a page.                                 *
 4  **********************************************/
 5 #define PAPER_WIDTH 8.5; // Width of the page
 6 #define MARGIN      1.0; // Total margins
 7 // Usable space on the page
 8 #define USABLE      PAPER_WIDTH -MARGIN;
 9
10 #include <iostream>
11
12 int main()
13 {
14     // The usable width
15     double text_width = USABLE;
16
17     std::cout << "Text width is " <<
18         text_width << '\n';
19     return (0);
20 }
```

(Next Hint 45. Answer 82.)

In my off-hours, I ported the game Adventure to the company computer and spent more than a few odd hours playing my game. One morning my manager called me into his office.

"Did you put Adventure on the system?" he asked.

"I did it my off-hours," I replied.

"Oh, I'm not criticizing you," he assured me. "As a matter of fact, I want to commend you. Ever since this project began, we've had daily visits from Bill (the head of marketing). Every day he comes in, plays with the software, and then insists on changes. But in the past week, he's spent all his time playing Adventure, giving him no time to make change requests. I just wanted to thank you for keeping him out of my hair."

Program 79: Square Deal

C++ doesn't have a power operator, so we define our own macro to compute X^2. We've decided to test this macro by printing the squares of the numbers from 1 to 10. But what do we really print?

```
1  /*********************************************
2   * Print out the square of the numbers        *
3   *      from 1 to 10.                          *
4   *********************************************/
5  #include <iostream>
6
7  /*********************************************
8   * macro to square a number.                  *
9   *********************************************/
10 #define SQR(x) ((x) * (x))
11
12 int main()
13 {
14     int number; // The number we are squaring
15
16     number = 1;
17
18     while (number <= 10) {
19         std::cout << number << " squared is " <<
20             SQR(++number) << std::endl;
21     }
22
23     return (0);
24 }
```

(Next Hint 200. Answer 88.)

Program 80: Area Bombing

We need to compute the area of a rectangle. We have the top in two parts and the side. But why does the following macro report an incorrect area?

```
 1 /*********************************************
 2 * Find the area of a rectangle.   The top of  *
 3 * the rectangle consists of two parts,        *
 4 * cleverly called PART1 and PART2.            *
 5 * The side is called SIDE.                    *
 6 *                                             *
 7 * So our rectangle looks like:                *
 8 *  <- TOP_PART1 ->|<-- TOP_PART2 ->|          *
 9 * +-------------------------------+ ^         *
10 * |                               | |         *
11 * |                               | |         *
12 * |                               | | SIDE    *
13 * |                               | |         *
14 * |                               | |         *
15 * +-------------------------------+ v         *
16 *********************************************/
17
18 // First leg of top is 37 feet
19 #define TOP_PART1 37
20
21 // Second part of the top is 33 feet
22 #define TOP_PART2 33
23
24 // Total top size
25 #define TOP_TOTAL TOP_PART1 + TOP_PART2
26
27 #define SIDE 10          // 10 Feet on a side
28
29 // Area of the rectangle
30 #define AREA TOP_TOTAL * SIDE
31
32 #include <iostream>
33
34 int main() {
35     std::cout << "The area is " <<
36         AREA << std::endl;
37     return (0);
38 }
```

(Next Hint 28. Answer 29.)

This page isn't intentionally left blank.

7

CLASSES WITH NO CLASS

When Bjarne Stroustrup invented C++, he not only created a great programming language, but he created a great language that gave the programmer tremendous power. He also gave the programmer an entirely new set of ways of screwing up. Thanks to his effort all the programs in this chapter are possible.

Program 81: Thanks for the Memory

Why does this program leak memory?

```
1  /**********************************************
2   * play with a variable size stack class.     *
3   **********************************************/
4
5  /**********************************************
6   * stack -- Simple stack class                *
7   *                                            *
8   * Member functions:                          *
9   *     push -- Push data on to the stack      *
10  *     pop -- remove an item from the stack.  *
11  **********************************************/
12 class stack
13 {
14     private:
15         int *data;      // The data
16         const int size; // The size of the data
17
18         // Number of items in the data
19         int count;
20     public:
21         // Create the stack
22         stack(
23             // Max size of the stack
24             const int _size
25         ):size(_size), count(0)
26         {
27             data = new int[size];
28         }
29         ~stack(void) {}
30     private:
31         // No copy constructor
32         stack(const stack &);
33
34         // No assignment operator
35         stack & operator = (const stack &);
```

```
36      public:
37          // Push something on the stack
38          void push(
39              // Value to put on stack
40              const int value
41          )
42          {
43              data[count] = value;
44              ++count;
45          }
46          // Remove an item from the stack
47          int pop(void)
48          {
49              --count;
50              return (data[count]);
51          }
52 };
53
54 int main()
55 {
56      stack a_stack(30);
57
58      a_stack.push(1);
59      a_stack.push(3);
60      a_stack.push(5);
61      a_stack.push(7);
62      return (0);
63 }
```

(Next Hint 56. Answer 32.)

Program 82: The Case of the Disappearing Array

We have a simple array class and an even simpler test routine. Yet somehow memory gets corrupted.

```
1  /**********************************************
2   * var_array -- Test variable length array     *
3   *      class.                                  *
4   **********************************************/
5  #include <memory.h>
6
7  /**********************************************
8   * var_array -- Variable length array          *
9   *                                             *
10  * Member functions:                           *
11  *      operator [] -- Return a reference to    *
12  *              the item in the array.          *
13  **********************************************/
14
15 class var_array
16 {
17     private:
18         int *data;      // The data
19         const int size; // The size of the data
20     public:
21         // Create the var_array
22         var_array(const int _size):
23             size(_size)
24         {
25             data = new int[size];
26             memset(data, '\0',
27                     size * sizeof(int));
28         }
29         // Destroy the var_array
30         ~var_array(void) {
31             delete []data;
32         }
33     public:
34         // Get an item in the array
35         int &operator [] (
36             // Index into the array
37             const unsigned index
38         )
39         {
40             return (data[index]);
41         }
```

```
42 };
43
44 /***********************************************
45 * store_it -- Store data in the var_array       *
46 ***********************************************/
47 static void store_it(
48     // Array to use for storage
49     var_array test_array
50 )
51 {
52     test_array[1] = 1;
53     test_array[3] = 3;
54     test_array[5] = 5;
55     test_array[7] = 7;
56 }
57 int main()
58 {
59     var_array test_array(30);
60
61     store_it(test_array);
62     return (0);
63 }
```

(Next Hint 189. Answer 59.)

Oualline's Law of Documentation

90 percent of the time, the documentation will be lost. Of the remaining 10 percent, 9 percent of the time it will be for an earlier version of the program and therefore completely useless. The 1 percent of the time you have the documentation and the correct revision of the documentation, it will be written in Japanese.

I told this joke to a fellow working at Motorola and he laughed for a few minutes, then pulled out his manual to Hitachi FORTRAN, written in Japanese.

Program 83: Wild Output

A student of C++ wanted to see how constructors and destructors were called, so he wrote the following program. Yet he learned more than he bargained for. What's the problem?

```
 1 /**********************************************
 2  * Class tester.   Test constructor / destructor*
 3  *       calling.                              *
 4  **********************************************/
 5 #include <iostream>
 6
 7 /**********************************************
 8  * tester -- Class that tells the world when   *
 9  *       it's created and destroyed.           *
10  **********************************************/
11 class tester {
12     public:
13         tester(void) {
14             std::cout <<
15                 "tester::tester() called\n";
16         }
17         ~tester(void) {
18             std::cout <<
19                 "tester::~tester() called\n";
20         }
21 };
22
23 static tester a_var;    // Variable to test with
24
25 int main()
26 {
27     std::cout << "In main\n";
28     return (0);
29 }
```

(Next Hint 157. Answer 111.)

Program 84: Construction Project

The student wanted to see when the copy constructor and the operator = were called, so he wrote this program. But the results surprised him. What's happening?

```
 1 #include <iostream>
 2 /**********************************************
 3  * trouble -- A class designed to store a     *
 4  *       single data item.                     *
 5  *                                             *
 6  * Member function:                            *
 7  *       put -- put something in the class      *
 8  *       get -- get an item from the class      *
 9  **********************************************/
10 class trouble {
11     private:
12         int data;        // An item to be stored
13     public:
14         trouble(void) { data = 0; }
15
16         trouble(const trouble &i_trouble) {
17             std::cout << "Copy Constructor called\n";
18             *this = i_trouble;
19         }
20         trouble operator = (const trouble &i_trouble) {
21             std::cout << "= operator called\n";
22             data = i_trouble.data;
23             return (*this);
24         }
25     public:
26         // Put an item in the class
27         void put(const int value) {
28             data = value;
29         }
30         // Get an item from the class
31         int get(void) {
32             return (data);
33         }
34 };
35
```

```
36 int main() {
37     trouble first;        // A place to put an item
38     first.put(99);
39
40     trouble second(first); // A copy of this space
41
42     std::cout << "Second.get " << second.get() << '\n';
43
44     return (0);
45 }
```

(Next Hint 291. Answer 109.)

Real Programmers don't comment their code. If it was hard to write, it should be hard to understand.

Real Programmers don't draw flowcharts. Flowcharts are, after all, the illiterate's form of documentation. Cavemen drew flowcharts; look how much good it did them.

Real Programmers don't play tennis, or any other sport that requires you to change clothes. Mountain climbing is okay, and Real Programmers wear their climbing boots to work in case a mountain should suddenly spring up in the middle of the machine room.

Real Programmers don't write in BASIC. Actually, no programmers write in BASIC after reaching puberty.

Real Programmers don't write specs — users should consider themselves lucky to get any programs at all and take what they get.

Real Programmers don't comment their code. If it was hard to write, it should be hard to understand.

Real Programmers don't write application programs; they program right down on the bare metal. Application programming is for feebs who can't do systems programming.

Real Programmers don't eat quiche. In fact, Real Programmers don't know how to SPELL quiche. They eat Twinkies and Szechwan food.

Program 85: Queueing Up Too Long

This program creates a very simple, well-formed queue class. Yet when we use it, memory gets corrupted. Why?

```
1  /*********************************************
2   * test the variable length queue class.       *
3   *********************************************/
4  #include <iostream>
5
6  /*********************************************
7   * queue -- Variable length queue class.        *
8   *                                              *
9   * Member functions:                            *
10  *       queue(size) -- Create a queue that can *
11  *               hold up to size elements.      *
12  *                                              *
13  *       get -- Return an item from the queue.  *
14  *               (Elements are gotten in First  *
15  *               In First Out (FIFO) order.)    *
16  *       put -- Add an item to the queue.       *
17  *                                              *
18  * WARNING: No safety check is made to make     *
19  * sure something is in the queue before        *
20  * it is removed.                               *
21  *********************************************/
22 class queue
23 {
24     private:
25         int *data;       // The data
26         int in_index;    // Input index
27         int out_index;   // Output index
28         int size;        // # items in the queue
29
30         // Copy data from another queue to me.
31         void copy_me(
32             // Stack to copy from
33             const queue &other
34         )
35         {
36             int i;       // Current element
37
38             for (i = 0; i < size; ++i) {
39                 data[i] = other.data[i];
40             }
41         }
```

```
42
43        // Inc_index -- Increment an
44        // index with wrapping
45        void inc_index(int &index)
46        {
47            ++index;
48            if (index == size)
49            {
50                // Wrap
51                index = 0;
52            }
53        }
54
55    public:
56        // Create a queue of the given size
57        queue(const int _size):
58            in_index(0), out_index(0), size(_size)
59        {
60            data = new int[size];
61        }
62
63        // Destructor
64        ~queue(void) {}
65
66        // Copy constructor
67        queue(const queue &other):
68            in_index(other.in_index),
69            out_index(other.out_index),
70            size(other.size)
71        {
72            data = new int[size];
73            copy_me(other);
74        }
75        // Assignment operator
76        queue & operator = (const queue &other)
77        {
78            copy_me(other);
79            return (*this);
80        };
81    public:
82        // Put an item on the queue
83        void put(
84            // Value to Put on the queue
85            const int value
86        )
87        {
88            data[in_index] = value;
```

```
89              inc_index(in_index);
90          }
91          // Return first element from the queue
92          int get(void)
93          {
94              // Value to return
95              int value = data[out_index];
96
97              inc_index(out_index);
98              return (value);
99          }
100 };
101
102 int main()
103 {
104     // Queue to play around with
105     queue a_queue(30);
106
107     // Loop counter for playing with the queue
108     int i;
109
110     for (i = 0; i < 30; ++i)
111         a_queue.put(i);
112
113     // Create a new queue, same as the current one
114     queue save_queue(20);
115     save_queue = a_queue;
116
117     std::cout << "Value is " <<
118         a_queue.get() << std::endl;
119
120     std::cout << "Value is " <<
121         a_queue.get() << std::endl;
122
123     std::cout << "Value is " <<
124         a_queue.get() << std::endl;
125
126     std::cout << "Value is " <<
127         a_queue.get() << std::endl;
128
129     return (0);
130 }
```

(Next Hint 334. Answer 14.)

Program 86: Lack of Self-Awareness

The following program is designed to test out our simple array. Yet there's a problem that causes the program to fail in an unexpected way.

```
1  /**********************************************
2   * array_test -- Test the use of the array class*
3   **********************************************/
4  #include <iostream>
5
6  /**********************************************
7   * array -- Classic variable length array class.*
8   *                                             *
9   * Member functions:                           *
10  *       operator [] -- Return an item          *
11  *                in the array.                 *
12  **********************************************/
13 class array {
14     protected:
15         // Size of the array
16         int size;
17
18         // The array data itself
19         int *data;
20     public:
21         // Constructor.
22         // Set the size of the array
23         // and create data
24         array(const int i_size):
25             size(i_size),
26             data(new int[size])
27         {
28             // Clear the data
29             memset(data, '\0',
30                     size * sizeof(data[0]));
31         }
32         // Destructor -- Return data to the heap
33         virtual ~array(void)
34         {
35             delete []data;
36             data = NULL;
37         }
```

```
38          // Copy constructor.
39          // Delete the old data and copy
40          array(const array &old_array)
41          {
42              delete []data;
43              data = new int[old_array.size];
44
45              memcpy(data, old_array.data,
46                      size * sizeof(data[0]));
47          }
48          // operator =.
49          // Delete the old data and copy
50          array & operator = (
51                  const array &old_array)
52          {
53              delete []data;
54              data = new int[old_array.size];
55
56              memcpy(data, old_array.data,
57                      size * sizeof(data[0]));
58              return (*this);
59          }
60      public:
61          // Get a reference to an item in the array
62          int &operator [](const unsigned int item)
63          {
64              return data[item];
65          }
66 };
67
68 /***********************************************
69 * three_more_elements  --                     *
70 *      Copy from_array to to_array and         *
71 *      put on three more elements.             *
72 ***********************************************/
73 void three_more_elements(
74      // Original array
75      array to_array,
76
77      // New array with modifications
78      const array &from_array
79 )
80 {
81      to_array = from_array;
82      to_array[10] = 1;
83      to_array[11] = 3;
84      to_array[11] = 5;
```

```
85 }
86 int main()
87 {
88     array an_array(30);  // Simple test array
89
90     an_array[2] = 2;     // Put in an element
91     // Put on a few more
92     three_more_elements(an_array, an_array);
93     return(0);
94 }
```

(Next Hint 8. Answer 75.)

A programmer at IBM's Yorktown Heights Research Center had a problem. When he was sitting down, everything went fine. When he stood up, the computer failed. Now this problem was interesting in that it was completely repeatable. When he stood up, the machine always failed, and when he sat down it always worked. Nothing flaky about this problem.

The people in the computer office were baffled. After all, how could the computer know when the guy was standing or sitting? All sorts of theories were floated, such as static electricity, magnetic fields, and even acts of a playful God.

The most likely theory was that there was something loose under the carpet. It was a nice theory, but unfortunately it didn't fit the facts. Loose wires tend to cause intermittent problems, but this was 100 percent reproducible.

Finally a sharp-eyed engineer noticed something. When the programmer sat down, he touch typed. When he stood up, he used the hunt and peck method. A careful examination of the keyboard revealed that two of the keys had been reversed. This didn't matter when the fellow sat down and touch-typed. But when he rose and used the hunt-and-peck method, he was misled by the reversed keys and input the wrong data.

When the key caps were switched, the problem went away.

Program 87: Exceptional Exception

This stack class is designed to be more robust and throws an exception if anything goes wrong with the stack. Yet the test program still aborts and dumps core. Why?

```
1 /**********************************************
2 * stack_test -- Yet another testing of a     *
3 *       stack class.                          *
4 **********************************************/
5 #include <iostream>
6
7 /**********************************************
8 * problem -- Class to hold a "problem".   Used *
9 *       for exception throwing and catching.  *
10 *                                             *
11 * Holds a single string which describes the   *
12 * error.                                      *
13 **********************************************/
14 class problem
15 {
16     public:
17         // The reason for the exception
18         char *what;
19
20         // Constructor.
21         // Create stack with messages.
22         problem(char *_what):what(_what){}
23 };
24
25 // Max data we put in a stack
26 // (private to the stack class)
27 const int MAX_DATA = 100;
28 /**********************************************
29 * stack -- Classic stack.                     *
30 *                                             *
31 * Member functions:                           *
32 *       push -- Push an item on the stack.     *
33 *       pop -- Remove an item from the stack.  *
34 *                                             *
35 * Exceptions:                                 *
36 *       Pushing too much data on a stack or    *
37 *       removing data from an empty stack      *
38 *       causes an exception of the "problem"   *
39 *       class to be thrown.                    *
40 *                                             *
```

```
41  *      Also if you don't empty a stack      *
42  *      before you're finished, an exception  *
43  *      is thrown.                            *
44  **********************************************/
45 class stack {
46    private:
47        // The stack's data
48        int data[MAX_DATA];
49
50        // Number of elements
51        // currently in the stack
52        int count;
53
54    public:
55        // Constructor
56        stack(void) : count(0) {};
57
58        // Destructor -- Check for non
59        ~stack(void)
60        {
61            if (count != 0)
62            {
63                throw(
64                    problem("Stack not empty"));
65            }
66        }
67
68        // Push an item on the stack
69        void push(
70            const int what      // Item to store
71        )
72        {
73            data[count] = what;
74            ++count;
75        }
76        // Remove an item from the stack
77        int pop(void)
78        {
79            if (count == 0)
80                throw(
81                    problem("Stack underflow"));
82        --count;
83            return (data[count]);
84        }
85 };
86
87 /**********************************************
```

```
88  * push_three -- Push three items onto a stack  *
89  *                                               *
90  * Exceptions:                                   *
91  *      If i3 is less than zero, a "problem"      *
92  *      class exception is thrown.               *
93  ************************************************/
94 static void push_three(
95     const int i1,      // First value to push
96     const int i2,      // Second value to push
97     const int i3       // Third value to push
98 )
99 {
100     // Stack on which to push things
101     stack a_stack;
102
103     a_stack.push(i1);
104     a_stack.push(i2);
105     a_stack.push(i3);
106     if (i3 < 0)
107         throw (problem("Bad data"));
108 }
109
110 int main(void)
111 {
112     try {
113         push_three(1, 3, -5);
114     }
115     catch (problem &info) {
116
117         std::cout << "Exception caught: " <<
118             info.what << std::endl;
119
120         exit (8);
121     }
122     catch (...) {
123         std::cout <<
124             "Caught strange exception " <<
125             std::endl;
126
127         exit (9);
128     }
129     std::cout << "Normal exit" << std::endl;
130     return (0);
131 }
```

(Next Hint 110. Answer 55.)

Program 88: File This!

Due to some brain-damaged program requirements, the following function must copy from a FILE to an ostream. Why does it fail to work?

```
1  /**********************************************
2   * copy -- Copy the input file to the output   *
3   *      file.                                   *
4   **********************************************/
5  #include <cstdio>
6  #include <iostream>
7  #include <fstream>
8
9  /**********************************************
10  * copy_it -- Copy the data                    *
11  **********************************************/
12 void copy_it(
13     FILE *in_file,      // Input file
14     std::ostream &out_file   // Output file
15 )
16 {
17     int ch;      // Current char
18
19     while (1) {
20         ch = std::fgetc(in_file);
21         if (ch == EOF)
22             break;
23         out_file << ch;
24     }
25 }
26
27 int main()
28 {
29     // The input file
30     FILE *in_file = std::fopen("in.txt", "r");
31     // The output file
32     std::ofstream out_file("out.txt");
33
34     // Check for errors
35     if (in_file == NULL) {
36         std::cerr <<
37             "Error: Could not open input\n";
38         exit (8);
39     }
```

```
40    if (out_file.bad()) {
41        std::cerr <<
42            "Error: Could not open output\n";
43        exit (8);
44    }
45    // Copy data
46    copy_it(in_file, out_file);
47
48    // Finish output file
49    std::fclose(in_file);
50    return (0);
51 }
```

(Next Hint 10. Answer 99.)

Error messages from an old Apple C compiler:

"Symbol table full - fatal heap error; please go buy a RAM upgrade from your local Apple dealer"

"String literal too long (1 let you have 512 characters, that's 3 more than ANSI said I should)"

"Type in (cast) must be scalar; ANSI 3.3.4; page 39, lines 10-11 (I know you don't care, I'm just trying to annoy you)"

"Too many errors on one line (make fewer)"

"Can't cast a void type to type void (because the ANSI spec. says so, that's why)"

". . . And the lord said, 'lo, there shall only be case or default labels inside a switch statement'"

"A typedef name was a complete surprise to me at this point in your program"

"'Volatile' and 'Register' are not miscible"

"You can't modify a constant, float upstream, win an argument with the IRS, or satisfy this compiler"

"This union already has a perfectly good definition"

"Huh?"

"Can't go mucking with a 'void *'"

"This struct already has a perfectly good definition"

"We already did this function"

"This label is the target of a goto from outside of the block containing this label AND this block has an automatic variable with an initializer AND your window wasn't wide enough to read this whole error message"

"Call me paranoid but finding '/*' inside this comment makes me suspicious"

Program 89: Just Because I'm Paranoid Doesn't Mean the Program Isn't Out to Get Me

In order to illustrate a problem with the setjmp library function, I created a v_string class. The test code for this function (minus the setjmp problem) is listed below.

Now I always try and code carefully to avoid errors and memory leaks. Yet this program failed because I was *too* careful. What's going on?

```
1  /*********************************************
2   * Combine strings with a variable length    *
3   *      string class.                         *
4   *********************************************/
5  #include <iostream>
6  #include <cstring>
7
8  /*********************************************
9   * v_string -- variable length C style string *
10  *                                            *
11  * Member functions:                          *
12  *      set -- set the value of the string.   *
13  *      get -- get the data from the string.  *
14  *********************************************/
15 class v_string
16 {
17     public:
18         const char *data;      // The data
19         // Default constructor
20         v_string(): data(NULL)
21         {}
22         v_string(const char *const i_data):
23             data(strdup(i_data))
24         {}
25         // Destructor
26         ~v_string(void)
27         {
28             // Note: delete works
29             // even if data is NULL
30             delete [] data;
31             data = NULL;
32         }
33         // Copy constructor
34         v_string(const v_string &old)
35         {
36             if (data != NULL)
37             {
```

```
38                 delete[] data;
39                 data = NULL;
40             }
41             data = strdup(old.data);
42         }
43         // operator =
44         v_string & operator = (
45                 const v_string &old)
46         {
47             if (this == &old)
48                 return (*this);
49
50             if (data != NULL)
51             {
52                 delete[] data;
53                 data = NULL;
54             }
55             if (old.data == NULL)
56             {
57                 data = NULL;
58                 return (*this);
59             }
60
61             data = strdup(old.data);
62             return (*this);
63         }
64     public:
65         // Set a value
66         void set(
67             // New string value
68             const char *const new_data
69         )
70         {
71             if (data != NULL)
72             {
73                 delete [] data;
74                 data = NULL;
75             }
76             data = strdup(new_data);
77
78         }
79         // Returns the value of the string
80         const char * const get(void) const
81         {
82             return (data);
83         }
84 };
```

```
85  /***********************************************
86   * operator + -- Combine two v_strings         *
87   ***********************************************/
88  v_string operator + (
89          const v_string &first,   // First string
90          const v_string &second   // Second string
91  )
92  {
93      char tmp[100];        // Combined string
94
95      strcpy(tmp, first.get());
96      strcat(tmp, second.get());
97
98      // Strings put together
99      v_string together(tmp);
100     return (together);
101 }
102
103 /***********************************************
104  * combine -- Combine two strings and          *
105  *      print the result.                      *
106  ***********************************************/
107 static void combine(
108         const v_string &first,   // First string
109         const v_string &second   // Second string
110 )
111 {
112     v_string together;  // Strings put together
113     together = first + second;
114
115     std::cout << "Combination " <<
116         together.get() << '\n';
117 }
118
119 int main()
120 {
121     // Strings to combine
122     v_string first("First:");
123     v_string second("Second");
124     combine(first, second);
125     return (0);
126 }
```

(Next Hint 65. Answer 115.)

Program 90: It's As Easy As Rolling off a Log

In order to track a memory leak, our clever programmer decided to put in logging information into new and delete by redefining the global functions.

Although C++ allows this, his program still crashes. Why?

```
 1  /***********************************************
 2   * simple debugging library that overrides the  *
 3   * standard new and delete operators so that we *
 4   * log all results.                             *
 5   ***********************************************/
 6  #include <iostream>
 7  #include <fstream>
 8  #include <cstdlib>
 9
10  // Define the file to write the log data to
11  std::ofstream log_file("mem.log");
12
13  /***********************************************
14   * operator new -- Override the system new so   *
15   *      that it logs the operation.  This is     *
16   *      useful for debugging.                    *
17   *                                               *
18   * Note: We have verified that the real new      *
19   *      calls malloc on this system.             *
20   *                                               *
21   * Returns a pointer to the newly created area. *
22   ***********************************************/
23  void *operator new(
24      // Size of the memory to allocate
25      const size_t size
26  )
27  {
28      // Result of the malloc
29      void *result = (void *)malloc(size);
30
31      log_file <<
32          result << " =new(" <<
33          size << ")" << std::endl;
34
35      return (result);
36  }
37
```

```
38 /**********************************************
39  * operator delete -- Override the system       *
40  *      delete to log the operation.   This is   *
41  *      useful for debugging.                     *
42  *                                                *
43  * Note: We have verified that the real delete   *
44  *      calls free on this system.                *
45  **********************************************/
46 void operator delete(
47     void *data  // Data to delete
48 )
49 {
50     log_file << data << " Delete" << std::endl;
51     free (data);
52 }
53
54 // Dummy main
55 int main()
56 {
57     return (0);
58 }
```

(Next Hint 212. Answer 110.)

Law of advanced programming languages: Make it possible for programmers to write in English, and you will find the programmers cannot write in English.

Program 91: Stacked Wrong

In the following program we define an unsafe class, stack, and a safer version of it, safe_stack. Our test program creates an array of five stacks and pushes on some test data. It prints the size of the stack. But the results are not what we expect.

```
1  /**********************************************
2   * stack_test -- Test the use of the classes  *
3   *      stack and safe_stack.                  *
4   **********************************************/
5  #include <iostream>
6
7  // The largest stack we can use
8  // (private to class stack and safe_stack)
9  const int STACK_MAX = 100;
10 /**********************************************
11  * stack -- Class to provide a classic stack.  *
12  *                                             *
13  * Member functions:                           *
14  *      push -- Push data on to the stack.     *
15  *      pop -- Return the top item from the    *
16  *             stack.                          *
17  *                                             *
18  * Warning: There are no checks to make sure   *
19  *      that stack limits are not exceeded.    *
20  **********************************************/
21 class stack {
22     protected:
23         int count; // Number of items in the stack
24         int *data; // The stack data
25     public:
26         // Initialize the stack
27         stack(void): count(0)
28         {
29             data = new int[STACK_MAX];
30         }
31         // Destructor
32         virtual ~stack(void) {
33             delete data;
34             data = NULL;
35         }
36     private:
37         // No copy constructor
38         stack(const stack &);
39
```

```
40          // No assignment operator
41          stack & operator = (const stack &);
42      public:
43          // Push an item on the stack
44          void push(
45              const int item      // Item to push
46          ) {
47              data[count] = item;
48              ++count;
49          }
50          // Remove the an item from the stack
51          int pop(void) {
52              --count;
53              return (data[count]);
54          }
55
56          // Function to count things in
57          // an array of stacks
58          friend void stack_counter(
59              stack stack_array[],
60              const int n_stacks
61          );
62  };
63
64  /*********************************************
65   * safe_stack -- Like stack, but checks for   *
66   *      errors.                               *
67   *                                            *
68   * Member functions: push and pop             *
69   *              (just like stack)             *
70   *********************************************/
71  class safe_stack : public stack {
72      public:
73          const int max;  // Limit of the stack
74      public:
75          safe_stack(void): max(STACK_MAX) {};
76          // Destructor defaults
77      private:
78          // No copy constructor
79          safe_stack(const safe_stack &);
80
81          // No assignment operator
82          safe_stack & operator =
83              (const safe_stack &);
```

```
84     public:
85         // Push an item on the stack
86         void push(
87             // Data to push on the stack
88             const int data
89         ) {
90             if (count >= (STACK_MAX-1)) {
91                 std::cout << "Stack push error\n";
92                 exit (8);
93             }
94             stack::push(data);
95         }
96         // Pop an item off the stack
97         int pop(void) {
98             if (count <= 0) {
99                 std::cout << "Stack pop error\n";
100                exit (8);
101            }
102            return (stack::pop());
103        }
104 };
105
106
107 /**********************************************
108  * stack_counter -- Display the count of the    *
109  *      number of items in an array of stacks.  *
110  **********************************************/
111 void stack_counter(
112     // Array of stacks to check
113     stack *stack_array,
114
115     // Number of stacks to check
116     const int n_stacks
117 )
118 {
119     int i;
120
121     for (i = 0; i < n_stacks; ++i)
122     {
123         std::cout << "Stack " << i << " has " <<
124             stack_array[i].count << " elements\n";
125     }
126 }
127
```

```
128 // A set of very safe stacks for testing
129 static safe_stack stack_array[5];
130
131 int main()
132 {
133
134     stack_array[0].push(0);
135
136     stack_array[1].push(0);
137     stack_array[1].push(1);
138
139     stack_array[2].push(0);
140     stack_array[2].push(1);
141     stack_array[2].push(2);
142
143     stack_array[3].push(0);
144     stack_array[3].push(1);
145     stack_array[3].push(2);
146     stack_array[3].push(3);
147
148     stack_array[4].push(0);
149     stack_array[4].push(1);
150     stack_array[4].push(2);
151     stack_array[4].push(3);
152     stack_array[4].push(4);
153
154     stack_counter(stack_array, 5);
155     return (0);
156 }
```

(Next Hint 296. Answer 72.)

There is nothing that cannot be solved through sufficient application of brute force and ignorance.

Program 92: Name Game

What does the following program print?

File: first.cpp

```
1 #include <string>
2
3 // The first name of the key person
4 std::string first_name = "Bill";
```

File: last.cpp

```
1 /**********************************************
2  * print_name -- Print the name of a person.   *
3  **********************************************/
4 #include <iostream>
5 #include <string>
6
7 // The first name
8 extern std::string first_name;
9
10 // The last name
11 std::string last_name = "Jones";
12
13 // The full name
14 std::string full_name =
15     first_name + " " + last_name;
16
17 int main()
18 {
19     // Print the name
20     std::cout << full_name << std::endl;
21     return (0);
22 }
```

(Next Hint 244. Answer 3.)

After a number of decimal places, nobody gives a damn.

Program 93: No Magic

Something strange was happening to the class info. Your valiant author was assigned the task of figuring out what was happening. After a little playing around, I decided that what was probably happening is that someone had gotten a hold of a bad pointer and was stepping all over the class.

To try and find out where the class was being overwritten, I put a couple of magic numbers at the beginning and end of the data for the class. I expected these magic numbers to get changed when things went wrong. But I was surprised to learn that things went wrong much sooner than expected.

So why does the magic go out of the class?

```
 1 #include <stdlib.h>
 2 #include <iostream>
 3 #include <cstring>
 4
 5 /***********************************************
 6  * info -- A class to hold information.        *
 7  *                                             *
 8  * Note:                                       *
 9  *      Because someone is walking all over our *
10  *      memory  and destroying our data, we    *
11  *      have put two guards at the beginning   *
12  *      and end of our  class.   If someone    *
13  *      messes with us these numbers will      *
14  *      be destroyed.                          *
15  *                                             *
16  * Member functions:                           *
17  *      set_data -- Store a string in our data. *
18  *      get_data -- Get the data string.       *
19  *      check_magic -- Check the magic numbers. *
20  ***********************************************/
21 // Magic numbers for the start and end of the
22 // data in the class info
23 const int START_MAGIC = 0x11223344;
24 const int END_MAGIC = 0x5567788;
25 class info
26 {
27     private:
28         // Magic protection constant
29         const int start_magic;
30
31         // String to be stored
32         char data[30];
33
```

```cpp
34          // Magic protection constant
35          const int end_magic;
36      public:
37          info(void):
38              start_magic(START_MAGIC),
39              end_magic(END_MAGIC)
40              {}
41
42          // Copy constructor defaults
43          // Assignment operator defaults
44          // Destructor defaults
45
46          // Store some data in the class
47          void set_data(
48              // Data to be stored
49              const char what[]
50          )
51          {
52              strcpy(data, what);
53          }
54
55          // Get the data from the class
56          char *get_data(void)
57          {
58              return (data);
59          }
60
61          // Verify that the magic
62          // numbers are correct
63          void check_magic(void)
64          {
65              if ((start_magic != START_MAGIC) ||
66                  (end_magic != END_MAGIC))
67              {
68                  std::cout <<
69                      "Info has lost its magic\n";
70              }
71          }
72 };
73
```

```
74 /*********************************************
75  * new_info -- Create a new version of the    *
76  *        info class.                          *
77  *********************************************/
78 struct info *new_info(void)
79 {
80     struct info *result; // Newly created result.
81
82     result = (struct info *)
83         malloc(sizeof(struct info));
84
85     // Make sure the structure is clear
86     memset(result, '\0', sizeof(result));
87
88     return (result);
89 }
90 int main()
91 {
92     // An info class to play with
93     class info *a_info = new_info();
94
95     a_info->set_data("Data");
96     a_info->check_magic();
97     return (0);
98 }
```

(Next Hint 153. Answer 98.)

Profanity is the one language that all programmers understand.

Program 94: Speed Kills

The new and delete function calls are costly. If you want to speed up your program and you know what you are doing, you can override them and create your own class-specific new and delete. That's what this programmer has done. The allocation algorithm is surprising simple, yet somehow memory gets corrupted. Why?

```
 1 /**********************************************
 2 * bit_test -- Test out our new high speed      *
 3 *      bit_array.                               *
 4 **********************************************/
 5 #include <iostream>
 6 #include <memory.h>
 7
 8 // The size of a fast bit_array.
 9 // (Private to fast bit array)
10 const int BIT_ARRAY_MAX = 64;   // Size in bits
11
12 // Number of bits in a byte
13 const int BITS_PER_BYTE = 8;
14 /**********************************************
15 * fast_bit_array -- A bit array using fast     *
16 * allocate technology.                         *
17 *                                              *
18 * Member functions:                            *
19 *      get -- Get an element from the          *
20 *              array.                          *
21 *      set -- Set the value of an element      *
22 *              in the array.                   *
23 *                                              *
24 *      new -- used to quickly allocate a bit   *
25 *              array.                          *
26 *      delete -- used to quickly deallocate    *
27 *                  a bit array.                *
28 **********************************************/
29 class fast_bit_array
30 {
31     protected:
32         // Array data
33         unsigned char
34             data[BIT_ARRAY_MAX/BITS_PER_BYTE];
35
36     public:
37         fast_bit_array(void)
38         {
```

```
39            memset(data, '\0', sizeof(data));
40        }
41        // Destructor defaults
42    private:
43        // No copy constructor
44        fast_bit_array(const fast_bit_array &);
45
46        // No assignment operator
47        fast_bit_array & operator =
48            (const fast_bit_array &);
49    public:
50        // Set the value on an item
51        void set(
52            // Index into the array
53            const unsigned int index,
54
55            // Value to put in the array
56            const unsigned int value
57        )
58        {
59            // Index into the bit in the byte
60            unsigned int bit_index = index % 8;
61
62            // Byte in the array to use
63            unsigned int byte_index = index / 8;
64
65            if (value)
66            {
67                data[byte_index] |=
68                    (1 << bit_index);
69            }
70            else
71            {
72                data[byte_index] &=
73                    ~(1 << bit_index);
74            }
75        }
76        // Return the value of an element
77        int get(unsigned int index)
78        {
79            // Index into the bit in the byte
80            unsigned int bit_index = index % 8;
81            // Byte in the array to use
82            unsigned int byte_index = index / 8;
83
84            return (
85                (data[byte_index] &
```

```
86                          (1 << bit_index)) != 0);
87          }
88          // Allocate a new fast_bit_array
89          void *operator new(const size_t);
90
91          // Delete a fast bit array.
92          void operator delete(void *ptr);
93 };
94
95 /***********************************************
96 * The following routines handle the local     *
97 * new/delete for the fast_bit_array.           *
98 ***********************************************/
99 // Max number of fast_bit_arrays we can use at once
100 const int N_FAST_BIT_ARRAYS = 30;
101
102 // If true, the bit array slot is allocated
103 // false indicates a free slot
104 static bool
105     bit_array_used[N_FAST_BIT_ARRAYS] = {false};
106
107 // Space for our fast bit arrays.
108 static char
109     bit_array_mem[N_FAST_BIT_ARRAYS]
110                 [sizeof(fast_bit_array)];
111
112 // Handle new for "fast_bit_array".
113 // (This is much quicker than the
114 //      system version of new)
115 /***********************************************
116 * fast_bit_array -- new                        *
117 *                                              *
118 * This is a high speed allocation routine for  *
119 * the fast_bit_array class.   The method used  *
120 * for this is simple, but we know that only    *
121 * a few bit_arrays will be allocated.          *
122 *                                              *
123 * Returns a pointer to the new memory.         *
124 ***********************************************/
125 void *fast_bit_array::operator new(const size_t)
126 {
127     int i;      // Index into the bit array slots
128
129     // Look for a free slot
130     for (i = 0; i < N_FAST_BIT_ARRAYS; ++i)
131     {
132         if (!bit_array_used[i])
```

```
133          {
134              // Free slot found, allocate the space
135              bit_array_used[i] = true;
136              return(bit_array_mem[i]);
137          }
138      }
139      std::cout << "Error: Out of local memory\n";
140      exit (8);
141 }
142
143 /***********************************************
144  * fast_bit_array -- delete                    *
145  *                                             *
146  * Quickly free the space used by a            *
147  * fast bit array.                             *
148  ***********************************************/
149 void fast_bit_array::operator delete(
150      void *ptr   // Pointer to the space to return
151 )
152 {
153      int i;      // Slot index
154
155      for (i = 0; i < N_FAST_BIT_ARRAYS; ++i)
156      {
157          // Is this the right slot
158          if (ptr == bit_array_mem[i])
159          {
160              // Right slot, free it
161              bit_array_used[i] = false;
162              return;
163          }
164      }
165      std::cout <<
166          "Error: Freed memory we didn't have\n";
167      exit (8);
168 }
169
170
171 /***********************************************
172  * safe_bit_array -- A safer bit array.        *
173  *                                             *
174  * Like bit array, but with error checking.    *
175  ***********************************************/
176 class safe_bit_array : public fast_bit_array
177 {
178      public:
179          // Sequence number generator
```

```
180        static int bit_array_counter;
181
182        // Our bit array number
183        int sequence;
184
185        safe_bit_array(void)
186        {
187            sequence = bit_array_counter;
188            ++bit_array_counter;
189        };
190        // Destructor defaults
191    private:
192        // No copy constructor
193        safe_bit_array(const safe_bit_array &);
194
195        // No assignment operator
196        safe_bit_array & operator = (
197                const safe_bit_array &);
198    public:
199        // Set the value on an item
200        void set(
201            // Where to put the item
202            const unsigned int index,
203            // Item to put
204            const unsigned int value
205        )
206        {
207            if (index >= (BIT_ARRAY_MAX-1))
208            {
209                std::cout <<
210                    "Bit array set error "
211                    "for bit array #"
212                    << sequence << "\n";
213                exit (8);
214            }
215            fast_bit_array::set(index, value);
216        }
217        // Return the value of an element
218        int get(unsigned int index)
219        {
220            if (index >= (BIT_ARRAY_MAX-1))
221            {
222                std::cout <<
223                    "Bit array get error "
224                    "for bit array #"
225                    << sequence << "\n";
226                exit (8);
```

```
227              }
228              return (fast_bit_array::get(index));
229         }
230 };
231
232 // Sequence information
233 int safe_bit_array::bit_array_counter = 0;
234
235 int main()
236 {
237     // Create a nice new safe bit array
238     safe_bit_array *a_bit_array =
239         new safe_bit_array;
240
241     a_bit_array->set(5, 1);
242     // Return the bit_array to the system
243     delete a_bit_array;
244     return (0);
245 }
```

(Next Hint 305. Answer 56.)

——————————————

A sufficiently high level of technology is indistinguishable from magic.
— Arthur C. Clarke

——————————————

Program 95: Sending the Wrong Message

Why does this program generate strange results?

```
 1 /**********************************************
 2  * hello -- write hello using our message system*
 3  *      to the log file and the screen.       *
 4  **********************************************/
 5 #include <iostream>
 6 #include <fstream>
 7
 8 // The log file
 9 std::ofstream log_file("prog.log");
10
11 /**********************************************
12  * print_msg_one -- Write a message to the    *
13  *      given file.                           *
14  **********************************************/
15 void print_msg_one(
16     // File to write the message to
17     std::ostream out_file,
18
19     // Where to send it
20     const char msg[]
21 ) {
22     out_file << msg << std::endl;
23 }
24 /**********************************************
25  * print_msg -- send a message to the console *
26  *      and to the log file.                  *
27  **********************************************/
28 void print_msg(
29     const char msg[]    // Message to log
30 ) {
31     print_msg_one(std::cout, msg);
32     print_msg_one(log_file, msg);
33 }
34 int main()
35 {
36     print_msg("Hello World!");
37     return (0);
38 }
```

(Next Hint 328. Answer 40.)

Program 96: Pure Fun

This program is based on a simple idea. Let the list class handle the linked list and the derived classes handle the data.

But when it's run, it bombs. Why?

```
1  /**********************************************
2   * simple linked list test.                  *
3   **********************************************/
4  #include <iostream>
5  #include <malloc.h>
6  #include <string>
7  /**********************************************
8   * list -- Linked list class.                *
9   *        Stores a pointer to void so you can *
10  *        stick any data you want to in it.   *
11  *                                            *
12  * Member functions:                          *
13  *        clear -- clear the list             *
14  *        add_node -- Add an item to the list *
15  **********************************************/
16 class list {
17     private:
18         /*
19          * Node -- A node in the linked list
20          */
21         class node {
22             private:
23                 // Data for this node
24                 void *data;
25
26                 // Pointer to next node
27                 class node *next;
28
29                 // List class does the work
30                 friend class list;
31                 // Constructor defaults
32                 // Destructor defaults
33
34                 // No copy constructor
35                 node(const node &);
36
37                 // No assignment operator
38                 node &operator = (const node &);
39             public:
40                 node(void) :
```

```
41                    data(NULL), next(NULL) {}
42        };
43        //------------------------------------------
44
45        node *first;    // First node in the list
46
47        /*
48         * Delete the data for the node.
49         * Because we don't know what type of
50         * data we have,the derived class does
51         * the work of deleting the data
52         * through the delete_data function.
53         */
54        virtual void delete_data(void *data) = 0;
55    public:
56        // Delete all the data in the list
57        void clear(void) {
58            while (first != NULL)
59            {
60                // Pointer to the next node
61                class node *next;
62
63                next = first->next;
64                delete_data(first->data);
65                delete first;
66                first = next;
67            }
68        }
69
70        // Constructor
71        list(void): first(NULL) {};
72
73        // Destructor.  Delete all data
74        virtual ~list(void) {
75            clear();
76        }
77
78        // Add a node to the list
79        void add_node(
80            void *data  // Data to be added
81        ) {
82            class node *new_node;
83
84            new_node = new node;
85            new_node->data = data;
86            new_node->next = first;
87            first = new_node;
```

```
 88            }
 89 };
 90 /**********************************************
 91  * string_list -- A linked list containing    *
 92  *         strings.                            *
 93  *                                             *
 94  * Uses the list class to provide a linked list *
 95  * of strings.                                 *
 96  *                                             *
 97  * Member functions:                           *
 98  *         add_node -- Adds a node to the list. *
 99  **********************************************/
100 class string_list : private list
101 {
102     private:
103         // Delete a node
104         void delete_data(
105             void *data          // Data to delete
106         ) {
107             free(data);
108             data = NULL;
109         }
110     public:
111         // Add a new node to the list
112         void add_node(
113             // String to add
114             const char *const data
115         ) {
116             list::add_node((void *)strdup(data));
117         }
118 };
119
120 int main()
121 {
122     // List to test things with
123     string_list *the_list = new string_list;
124
125     the_list->add_node("Hello");
126     the_list->add_node("World");
127
128     delete the_list;
129     the_list = NULL;
130     return (0);
131 }
```

(Next Hint 119. Answer 101.)

8

EXPERT CONFUSION

Welcome to one of the toughest parts of the book. The few programs in this section are designed to baffle even the most expert C or C++ programmer. You may think you know all about programming, but the problems presented next are the toughest, most difficult ones around.

There are only three problems in this chapter. If you get one you can consider yourself an expert. Get two, and I'll be amazed. Get all three, and you can consider yourself a champion.

Program 97: Hello Again

What does the following program print?

```
1  /*********************************************
2   * Normally I would put in a comment explaining *
3   * what this program is nominally used for.      *
4   * But in this  case I can figure out no         *
5   * practical use for this program.               *
6   *********************************************/
7  #include <stdio.h>
8  #include <unistd.h>
9  #include <stdlib.h>
10
11 int main()
12 {
13     printf("Hello ");
14     fork();
15     printf("\n");
16     exit(0);
17 }
```

(Next Hint 214. Answer 50.)

Shakespeare has given us the age-old question, "To be or not to be?" Computer science has given us the answer: "FF".

```
0x2B | ~0x2B == 0xFF
```

NOTE *Most of the time when I tell this joke to non-technical people, they just look at me strangely. Technical people tend to think for a minute and then say, "You're right." Only one person in about a hundred actually laughs.*

Program 98: Debug Resistant

The programmer had a clever idea. He would put a bunch of code in an:

```
if (debugging)
```

statement. He would then run the program and when he wanted debugging output, he would use the interactive debugger to change debugging from 0 to 1. But his code was about to surprise him.

```
 1 /*********************************************
 2  * Code fragment to demonstrate how to use the  *
 3  * debugger to turn on debugging.   All you      *
 4  * have to do is put a breakpoint on the "if"    *
 5  * line and change the debugging variable.       *
 6  *********************************************/
 7 extern void dump_variables(void);
 8
 9 void do_work()
10 {
11     static int debugging = 0;
12
13     if (debugging)
14     {
15         dump_variables();
16     }
17     // Do real work
18 }
```

(Next Hint 147. Answer 84.)

Making files is easy under the UNIX operating system. Therefore, users tend to create numerous files using large amounts of file space. It has been said that the only standard thing about all UNIX systems is the message of the day telling users to clean up their files.

— Early UNIX administrator's guide

Program 99: Phantom File

There's no file named *delete.me* in our directory. So why does this program keep telling us to remove it?

```
 1 /*********************************************
 2  * delete_check -- Check to see if the file   *
 3  *      delete.me exists and tell the user    *
 4  *      to delete it if it does.              *
 5  *********************************************/
 6 #include <iostream>
 7 #include <unistd.h>
 8 #include <cstdio>
 9
10 int main()
11 {
12     // Test for the existence of the file
13     if (access("delete.me", F_OK)) {
14         bool remove = true;
15     }
16     if (remove) {
17         std::cout <<
18             "Please remove 'delete.me'\n";
19     }
20     return (0);
21 }
```

(Next Hint 98. Answer 35.)

Wherein I spake of most disastrous changes,
Of moving accidents by flood and field,
Of hair-breath 'scapes i' the imminent deadly breath.
— Shakespeare, on porting programming

Bloody instruction which, being learned, return to plague the
inventor.
— Shakespeare, on maintenance programming

9

PORTAGE TO HELL

C++ is supposed to be a portable language. It's a lovely phrase, "supposed to be": It explains how we were able to find all the programs for this chapter.

Program 100: Going Down to Rio

The Rio is an MP3 music player. I worked on some Linux software for this device. Each data block ends with a 16-byte control structure. I carefully laid out the struct statement to make sure that the block structure was correct, yet when I tested the program, my Rio kept losing blocks.

So what is going on?

```
1  /*********************************************
2   * A small part of a set of routines to        *
3   * download music to a RIO mp3 player.          *
4   *                                              *
5   * Full sources for the original can be found   *
6   *      at http://www.oualline.com.             *
7   *                                              *
8   * This just tests the writing of the end of    *
9   * block structure to the device.               *
10  *********************************************/
11
12 #include <stdio.h>
13 /*
14  * The 16 byte end of block structure for a Rio.
15  *    (We'd label the fields if we knew what they
16  *    were.)
17  */
18 struct end_block_struct
19 {
20     unsigned long int next_512_pos;     // [0123]
21     unsigned char next_8k_pos1;         // [4]
22     unsigned char next_8k_pos2;         // [5]
23
24     unsigned long int prev_251_pos;     // [6789]
25     unsigned char prev_8k_pos1;         // [10]
26     unsigned char prev_8k_pos2;         // [11]
27
28     unsigned short check_sum;           // [12,13]
29     unsigned short prev_32K_pos;        // [14,15]
30 };
31
32 /*
33  * Macro to print offset of the
34  * field in the structure
35  */
36 #define OFFSET(what) \
37     printf(#what "      %d\n", int(&ptr->what));
38
```

```
39 int main()
40 {
41     // A structure for debugging the structure
42     struct end_block_struct *ptr = NULL;
43
44     printf("Structure size %d\n",
45             sizeof(end_block_struct));
46     OFFSET(next_512_pos);
47     OFFSET(next_8k_pos1);
48     OFFSET(next_8k_pos2);
49
50     OFFSET(prev_251_pos);
51     OFFSET(prev_8k_pos1);
52     OFFSET(prev_8k_pos2);
53
54     OFFSET(check_sum);
55     OFFSET(prev_32K_pos);
56     return (0);
57 }
```

(Next Hint 343. Answer 103.)

One large university computerized its class scheduling. Some course titles had to be abbreviated to make them fit into the length limits placed on them by the computer. Most courses abbreviated well, however "Human Sexuality, Intermediate Course" turned into "Sex Int. Course."

Program 101: Point of No Return

Why does the following program write out a correct file on UNIX and a bad one on Microsoft Windows? The program writes out 128 characters, but Microsoft Windows contains 129. Why?

```
1  /*********************************************
2   * Create a test file containing binary data.   *
3   *********************************************/
4  #include <iostream>
5  #include <fstream>
6  #include <stdlib.h>
7
8  int main()
9  {
10     // current character to write
11     unsigned char cur_char;
12
13     // output file
14     std::ofstream out_file;
15
16     out_file.open("test.out", std::ios::out);
17     if (out_file.bad())
18     {
19         std::cerr << "Can not open output file\n";
20         exit (8);
21     }
22
23     for (cur_char = 0;
24          cur_char < 128;
25          ++cur_char)
26     {
27         out_file << cur_char;
28     }
29     return (0);
30 }
```

(Next Hint 349. Answer 5.)

To err is human; to really foul up you need a computer. To keep things
fouled up you need a bureaucracy.

Program 102: Zipping Along

On most UNIX systems, this program works. On MS-DOS, it does not. Why?

```
1  /*********************************************
2   * Check a couple of zip codes.              *
3   *********************************************/
4  #include <iostream>
5
6  int main()
7  {
8      // A couple of zip codes
9      const int cleveland_zip   = 44101;
10     const int pittsburgh_zip  = 15201;
11
12     if (cleveland_zip < pittsburgh_zip)
13     {
14         std::cout <<
15             "Cleveland < Pittsburgh (Wrong)\n";
16     }
17     else
18     {
19         std::cout <<
20             "Pittsburgh < Cleveland (Right)\n";
21     }
22
23     return (0);
24 }
```

(Next Hint 104. Answer 104.)

A programmer once worked on a form letter generation program for a bank. The bank wanted to send out a special, personalized letter to its richest 1,000 customers. Unfortunately for the programmer, he didn't adequately debug his code. Even worse, the bank didn't check the first batch of form letters.

The result: The wealthiest 1,000 customers all got a letter that began, "Dear Rich Bastard."

10

A FEW WORKING PROGRAMS

Programmers love tricks. In this chapter, we take a look at some working programs that use extremely clever tricks to get the job done.

One interesting thing about these algorithms is that in the wild, they all existed totally without comments, thus giving all the programmers that followed a chance to puzzle them out for themselves. Now it's your turn.

Program 103: Quick Change

What's the quickest way to do the following:

> The variable i has the value 2 or 1. If i is 2 change it to 1. If i is 1 change it to 2.

(Next Hint 134. Answer 48.)

━━━━━━━━━━━━━━━━━━━━━━━━━━━━━━

There is a contest held every year called the Obfuscated C Contest. The contestants try to figure out how to write the most difficult and hard-to-read program possible. After all, they're programmers, and they know programs hard to understand under the best of circumstances. This contest gives them a chance to understand a program under the worst of circumstances.

Some of the awards have interesting titles:

BEST SIMPLE TASK PERFORMED IN A COMPLEX WAY.
BEST NONSIMPLE TASK PERFORMED IN A COMPLEX WAY.
MOST ILLEGIBLE CODE.
MOST WELL ROUNDED IN CONFUSION.
BEST RESEMBLANCE TO RANDOM TYPING ON THE KEYBOARD.
WORST ABUSE OF THE RULES.
STRANGEST SOURCE LAYOUT.
BEST ABUSE OF ANSI C.

━━━━━━━━━━━━━━━━━━━━━━━━━━━━━━

Program 104: Nothing Special

What's the purpose of the funny `if` statement in the subroutine below? It looks totally useless:

```
1  /************************************************
2   * sum_file -- Sum the first 1000 integers in   *
3   *        a file.                                *
4   ************************************************/
5  #include <iostream>
6  #include <fstream>
7  /************************************************
8   * get_data -- Get an integer from a file.      *
9   *                                              *
10  * Returns: The integer gotten from the file    *
12  ************************************************/
12 int get_data(
13     // The file containing the input
14     std::istream &in_file
15 ) {
16     int data;   // The data we just read
17     static volatile int seq = 0; // Data sequence number
19
19     ++seq;
20     if (seq == 500)
21         seq = seq;      // What's this for?
22
23     in_file.read(&data, sizeof(data));
24     return (data);
25 }
26
27 int main() {
28     int i;              // Data index
29     int sum = 0;        // Sum of the data so far
30
31     // The input file
32     std::ifstream in_file("file.in");
33
34     for (i = 0; i < 1000; ++i) {
35         sum = sum + get_data(in_file);
36     }
37     std::cout << "Sum is " << sum << '\n';
38     return (0);
39 }
```

(Next Hint 175. Answer 81.)

Program 105: Waving the Flag

One of the problems with cute tricks is that far too many programmers don't put in any comments that tell you what's going on. Here's a recreation of some code I found in the UNIX stty command. What's happening?

```
1 #include <stdio.h>
2
3 int main()
4 {
5     int flags = 0x5;    // Some sample flags
6
7     printf("-parity\n" + ((flags & 0x1) != 0));
8     printf("-break\n"  + ((flags & 0x2) != 0));
9     printf("-xon\n"    + ((flags & 0x4) != 0));
10    printf("-rts\n"    + ((flags & 0x8) != 0));
11    return (0);
12 }
13
```

(Next Hint 301. Answer 108.)

Ode to a Maintenance Programmer

Once more I travel that lone dark road
into someone else's impossible code
Through "if" and "switch" and "do" and "while"
that twist and turn for mile and mile
Clever code full of traps and tricks
and you must discover how it ticks
And then I emerge to ask anew,
"What the heck does this program do?"

11

THREADED, EMBEDDED — DREADED

When NASA attempted to launch the first space shuttle, they rolled the spacecraft out to the pad, put the astronauts on board, and started the countdown. Then the computer reported a self-check failure. They tried and tried and tried to figure out what was wrong. In the end, they had to cancel the launch.

The problem was eventually traced to a race condition that had a 1 out of 64 chance of occurring each time the system was started.

Programmers who have to deal with multiple processes and embedded systems have their own set of problems to worry about. These are usually much more difficult to find than ordinary errors because errors happen randomly, and bugs can resist discovery by testing. Furthermore, code that looks perfectly good and reasonable can contain hidden errors.

This chapter is devoted to the obscure, random, and fiendish bugs that plague the embedded programmer.

Program 106: Taking Out the Trash

We have a memory-mapped input port pointed to by in_port_ptr. The device can buffer up to three characters. In order to initialize the device, we need to empty the buffer and clear out any old garbage. That's what this function is supposed to do. But sometimes it doesn't work. Why?

```
1  /**********************************************
2   * clear port -- Clear the input port.         *
3   **********************************************/
4  // Input register
5  char *in_port_ptr  = (char *)0xFFFFFFE0;
6
7  // Output register
8  char *out_port_ptr = (char *)0xFFFFFFE1;
9
10 /**********************************************
11  * clear_input -- Clear the input device by    *
12  *      reading enough characters to empty the  *
13  *      buffer. (It doesn't matter if we read   *
14  *      extra, just so long as we read enough.) *
15  **********************************************/
16 void clear_input(void)
17 {
18     char ch;     // Dummy character
19
20     ch = *in_port_ptr;  // Grab data
21     ch = *in_port_ptr;  // Grab data
22     ch = *in_port_ptr;  // Grab data
23 }
```

(Next Hint 129. Answer 9.)

The First Rule of Program Optimization:
Don't do it.
The Second Rule of Program Optimization:
Don't do it yet.

Program 107: Better Trash Collector

We've fixed Program 106 by adding the keyword "volatile." But things still don't work right.

```
1  /***********************************************
2   * clear port -- Clear the input port.         *
3   ***********************************************/
4  // Input register
5  const char *volatile in_port_ptr  =
6          (char *)0xFFFFFFE0;
7
8  // Output register
9  const char *volatile out_port_ptr =
10         (char *)0xFFFFFFE1;
11
12 /***********************************************
13  * clear_input -- Clear the input device by    *
14  *      reading enough characters to empty the  *
15  *      buffer. (It doesn't matter if we read   *
16  *      extra, just so long as we read enough.) *
17  ***********************************************/
18 void clear_input(void)
19 {
20     char ch;     // Dummy character
21
22     ch = *in_port_ptr;  // Grab data
23     ch = *in_port_ptr;  // Grab data
24     ch = *in_port_ptr;  // Grab data
25 }
```

(Next Hint 336. Answer 61.)

A user called up technical support with a big problem. The technician tried for several hours to fix the problem over the phone but failed, so he asked the user to send him a copy of his disk. The next day, by Federal Express a letter arrived for the technician containing a photocopy of the disk. The user wasn't completely dumb: He knew that he had a two-sided disk, so he copied both sides.

Oddly enough, the technician was able to figure out what the problem was from the photocopy. Turns out the user had the wrong version of the software.

Program 108: Short Time

The programmer needed to create a precise short delay in his program. He discovered that if he did 1,863 multiplies, that would create the correct delay. This fact has been turned into the following subroutine. But in some circumstances, the function fails. Why?

```
 1 /***********************************************
 2  * bit_delay -- Delay one bit time for         *
 3  *      serial output.                          *
 4  *                                              *
 5  * Note: This function is highly system         *
 6  *      dependent.  If you change the           *
 7  *      processor or clock it will go bad.      *
 8  ***********************************************/
 9 void bit_delay(void)
10 {
11     int i;       // Loop counter
12     int result;  // Result of the multiply
13
14     // We know that 1863 multiplies delay
15     // the proper amount
16     for (i = 0; i < 1863; ++i)
17     {
18         result = 12 * 34;
19     }
20 }
```

(Next Hint 342. Answer 16.)

A real comment from one of my first programs.

```
C------------------------------------------------------------
C This program works just like PLOT10 except it works with
C metric data files (MDF). The reason that I didn't add a new
C format to PLOT10 was that PLOT10 is so convoluted that I
C can't understand it.
C
C I have no idea what the input units are nor do I have any idea
C what the output units are but I do know that if you divide
C by 3 the plots look about the right size.
C------------------------------------------------------------
```

Program 109: Short Time Revisited

The programmer attempted to fix Program 108 by changing the multiplication factors to variables. But the loop is still too short. What's happening?

```
 1 /**********************************************
 2 * bit_delay -- Delay one bit time for         *
 3 *       serial output.                         *
 4 *                                              *
 5 * Note: This function is highly system         *
 6 *       dependent.  If you change the          *
 7 *       processor or clock it will go bad.     *
 8 **********************************************/
 9 void bit_delay(void)
10 {
11     int i;      // Loop counter
12     int result; // Result of the multiply
13
14     // Factors for multiplication
15     int factor1 = 12;
16     int factor2 = 34;
17
18     // We know that 1863 multiples
19     // delay the proper amount
20     for (i = 0; i < 1863; ++i)
21     {
22         result = factor1 * factor2;
23     }
24 }
```

(Next Hint 107. Answer 89.)

I once received a cross-referencing program written in German. I had a translator work on it who knew German, but not programming. She translated "is called by" as "is shouted at."

Program 110: Short Time III

Program 109 has been fixed. Now the delay is closer to what we expect. Not exactly what we expect, but close. What's happening now?

```
 1 /*********************************************
 2  * bit_delay -- Delay one bit time for        *
 3  *      serial output.                         *
 4  *                                             *
 5  * Note: This function is highly system        *
 6  *      dependent.  If you change the          *
 7  *      processor or clock it will go bad.     *
 8  *********************************************/
 9 void bit_delay(void)
10 {
11     int i;       // Loop counter
12     volatile int result;// Result of the multiply
13
14     // Factors for multiplication
15     int factor1 = 12;
16     int factor2 = 34;
17
18     // We know that 1863 multiplies
19     // delay the proper amount
20     for (i = 0; i < 1863; ++i)
21     {
22         result = factor1 * factor2;
23     }
24 }
```

(Next Hint 95. Answer 39.)

---

1 is equal to 2 for sufficiently large values of 1.

Program 111: A Bump on the Race Track

This program starts two threads. One reads data into a buffer, and one writes the data to a file.

But the data gets corrupted sometimes. Why?

```
1  /**********************************************
2   * Starts two threads                        *
3   *                                           *
4   *      1) Reads data from /dev/input and puts *
5   *              it into a buffer.             *
6   *                                           *
7   *      2) Takes data from the buffer and     *
8   *              writes the data to /dev/output. *
9   **********************************************/
10 #include <cstdio>
11 #include <stdlib.h>
12 #include <pthread.h>
13 #include <unistd.h>
14 #include <sys/fcntl.h>
15
16 static const int BUF_SIZE = 1024;       // Buffer size
17 static char buffer[BUF_SIZE];           // The data buffer
18
19 // Pointer to end of buffer
20 static char *end_ptr = buffer + BUF_SIZE;
21
22 // Next character read goes here
23 static char *in_ptr = buffer;
24
25 // Next character written comes from here
26 static char *out_ptr = buffer;
27
28 static int count = 0;           // Number of characters in the buffer
29
30 /**********************************************
31  * reader -- Read data and put it in the global *
32  *      variable buffer.   When data is       *
33  *      installed the variable count is       *
34  *      increment and the buffer pointer      *
35  *      advanced.                             *
36  **********************************************/
37 static void *reader(void *) {
38     // File we are reading
39     int in_fd = open("/dev/input", O_RDONLY);
40
```

```
41     while (1) {
42         char ch; // Character we just got
43
44         while (count >= BUF_SIZE)
45             sleep(1);
46
47         read(in_fd, &ch, 1);
48
49         ++count;
50         *in_ptr = ch;
51         ++in_ptr;
52
53         if (in_ptr == end_ptr)
54             in_ptr = buffer;
55     }
56 }
57
58 /***********************************************
59  * writer -- Write data from the buffer to     *
60  *      the output device.   Gets the data     *
61  *      from the global buffer. Global variable *
62  *      count is decrement for each character  *
63  *      taken from the buffer and the buffer    *
64  *      pointer advanced.                       *
65  ***********************************************/
66 static void writer(void)
67 {
68     // Device to write to
69     int out_fd = open("/dev/output", O_RDONLY);
70
71     while (1) {
72         char ch;        // Character to transfer
73
74         while (count <= 0)
75             sleep(1);
76
77         ch = *out_ptr;
78
79         --count;
80         ++out_ptr;
81
82         if (out_ptr == end_ptr)
83             out_ptr = buffer;
84
85         write(out_fd, &ch, 1);
86     }
87 }
```

```
 88
 89 int main() {
 90     int status; /* Status of last system call */
 91
 92     /* Information on the status thread */
 93     pthread_t reader_thread;
 94
 95     status = pthread_create(&reader_thread, NULL, reader, NULL);
 96
 97     if (status != 0) {
 98         perror("ERROR: Thread create failed:\n    ");
 99         exit (8);
100     }
101
102     writer();
103     return (0);
104 }
```

(Next Hint 222. Answer 92.)

Over the years system installers have developed many different ways to string cables above false ceilings. One of the more innovative is the "small dog" method. One person takes a small dog, ties a string to its collar, and puts the dog in the ceiling. The owner then goes to the spot where they want the cable to come out and calls the dog. Dog runs to owner. They attach a cable to the string and pull it through, and the cable is installed.

Program 112: Hurry Up and Wait

For some reason this program runs for a while and then stops:

```
 1 #include <cstdio>
 2 #include <stdlib.h>
 3 #include <pthread.h>
 4 #include <sys/fcntl.h>
 5
 6 // Resource protection mutexes
 7 static pthread_mutex_t resource1 =
 8         PTHREAD_MUTEX_INITIALIZER;
 9
10 static pthread_mutex_t resource2 =
11         PTHREAD_MUTEX_INITIALIZER;
12
13 /*********************************************
14  * A couple of routines to do work.   Or they  *
15  *      would do work if we had any to do.     *
16  *********************************************/
17 static void wait_for_work(void) {}      // Dummy
18 static void do_work(void) {}            // Dummy
19
20 /*********************************************
21  * process_1 -- First process of two.          *
22  *                                             *
23  * Grab both resources and then do the work    *
24  *********************************************/
25 static void *process_1(void *)
26 {
27     while (1) {
28         wait_for_work();
29
30         pthread_mutex_lock(&resource1);
31         pthread_mutex_lock(&resource2);
32
33         do_work();
34
35         pthread_mutex_unlock(&resource2);
36         pthread_mutex_unlock(&resource1);
37     }
38 }
39
```

```
40 /*********************************************
41  * process_2 -- Second process of two.        *
42  *                                             *
43  * Grab both resources and then do the work.   *
44  *       (but slightly different work from      *
45  *        process_1)                            *
46  *********************************************/
47 static void process_2(void)
48 {
49     while (1) {
50         wait_for_work();
51
52         pthread_mutex_lock(&resource2);
53         pthread_mutex_lock(&resource1);
54
55         do_work();
56
57         pthread_mutex_unlock(&resource1);
58         pthread_mutex_unlock(&resource2);
59     }
60 }
61
62 int main()
63 {
64     int status; /* Status of last system call */
65
66     /* Information on the status thread */
67     pthread_t thread1;
68
69     status = pthread_create(&thread1,
70             NULL, process 1, NULL);
71
72     if (status != 0) {
73         perror(
74             "ERROR: Thread create failed:\n    ");
75         exit (8);
76     }
77
78     process_2();
79     return (0);
80 }
```

(Next Hint 97. Answer 24.)

Program 113: Flag Waving

This program contains a small part of the UNIX terminal driver. (The UNIX terminal driver uses lots and lots of flags.)

When this code was ported to a Celerity C1000 computer, we started to experience problems. About once a week, flags would be mysteriously set or cleared. Can you spot what is going on?

```
 1 /*********************************************
 2  * flag -- Demonstrate the use of flag setting  *
 3  *       and clearing.  This is a demonstration  *
 4  *       program that does not run in real life.  *
 5  *       But it is a good example of a very tiny  *
 6  *       part of the code in a terminal driver.   *
 7  *********************************************/
 8 #include <cstdio>
 9 #include <stdlib.h>
10 #include <pthread.h>
11
12
13 const char XOFF = 'S' - '@';// Turns off output
14 const char XON = 'Q' - '@'; // Turns on output
15
16 static int flags = 0;    // State flags
17 //
18 // ^S in effect
19 const int STOP_OUTPUT = (1 << 0);
20
21 // CD is present
22 const int CD_SIGNAL   = (1 << 1);
23
24 /*********************************************
25  * read_ch -- read a single character.          *
26  *                                              *
27  * Returns the character read.                  *
28  *********************************************/
29 static char read_ch(void)
30 {
31     // Dummy function
32     return ('x');
33 }
34
```

```
35  /***********************************************
36   * write_ch -- write a character to the output  *
37   *              (Whatever that is.)             *
38   ***********************************************/
39  static void write_ch(const char ch)
40  {
41      // Dummy function
42  }
43  /***********************************************
44   * do_input -- handle the reading and          *
45   *       processing of characters.             *
46   ***********************************************/
47  static void *do_input(void *)
48  {
49      while (1)
50      {
51          char ch;        // Character we just read
52
53          ch = read_ch();
54
55          switch (ch) {
56              case XOFF:
57                  flags |= STOP_OUTPUT;
58                  break;
59              case XON:
60                  flags &= ~STOP_OUTPUT;
61                  break;
62              default:
63                  write_ch(ch);
64                  break;
65          }
66      }
67  }
68
69  /***********************************************
70   * wait_for_cd_change -- wait for the CD signal *
71   *      to change and return the value of the   *
72   *      signal.                                 *
73   ***********************************************/
74  static int wait_for_cd_change(void)
75  {
76      // Dummy
77      return (1);
78  }
```

```
79 /**********************************************
80  * do_signals -- Monitor signals and set flags  *
81  *       based on the signal changes.           *
82  **********************************************/
83 void do_signals(void)
84 {
85     while (1) {
86         // The current cd level
87         int level = wait_for_cd_change();
88         if (level) {
89             flags |= CD_SIGNAL;
90         } else {
91             flags &= ~CD_SIGNAL;
92         }
93     }
94 }
95
96 int main()
97 {
98     int status; // Status of last system call
99
100     // Information on the status thread
101     pthread_t input_thread;
102
103     status = pthread_create(&input_thread,
104                 NULL, do_input, NULL);
105
106     if (status != 0) {
107         perror(
108             "ERROR: Thread create failed:\n    ");
109         exit (8);
110     }
111
112     do_signals();
113     return(0);
114 }
```

(Next Hint 22. Answer 52.)

The chief cause of problems is solutions.

Program 114: Slow Progress

This program consists of two threads. The first, sum, does some work that takes a lot of time. The second, status_monitor, displays a progress report every time the user hits the return key. But after a number of test runs, the programmer began to suspect that the status report was incorrect. Why?

```
1  /***********************************************
2   * Sum -- This program sums the sine of the    *
3   *        numbers from 1 to MAX. (For no good   *
4   *        reason other than to have something   *
5   *        to do that takes a long time.)        *
6   *                                              *
7   * Since this takes a long time, we have a      *
8   * second thread that displays the progress of  *
9   * the call.                                    *
10  ***********************************************/
11 #include <cstdio>
12 #include <cmath>
13 #include <pthread.h>
14 #include <stdlib.h>
15
16 /* Counter of what we've summed so far */
17 static int counter;
18
19 /***********************************************
20  * status_monitor -- Monitor the status and     *
21  *        tell the user how far things have      *
22  *        progressed.                            *
23  *                                              *
24  * This thread merely waits for the user to      *
25  * press <enter> and then reports the current    *
26  * value of counter.                             *
27  ***********************************************/
28 static void *status_monitor(void *) {
29     /* buffer to stuff that comes in */
30     char buffer[3];
31
32     while (1) {
33         fgets(buffer, sizeof(buffer), stdin);
34         printf("Progress %d\n", counter);
35         fflush(stdout);
36     }
37 }
38
```

```
39 /**********************************************
40  * sum -- Sum the sine of the numbers from 0 to *
41  *       0x3FFFFFFF.   Actually we don't care    *
42  *       about the answer, all we're trying to   *
43  *       do is create some sort of compute       *
44  *       bound job so that the status_monitor    *
45  *       can be demonstrated.                    *
46  **********************************************/
47 static void sum(void) {
48     static double sum = 0;       /* Sum so far */
49
50     for (counter = 0;
51          counter < 0x3FFFFFF;
52          ++counter)
53     {
54         sum += sin(double(counter));
55     }
56
57     printf("Total %f\n", sum);
58     exit (0);
59 }
60
61 int main() {
62     // Status of last system call
63     int status;
64
65     // Information on the status thread
66     pthread_t status_thread;
67
68     status = pthread_create(&status_thread, NULL,
69                 status_monitor, NULL);
70
71     if (status != 0) {
72         perror(
73             "ERROR: Thread create failed:\n    ");
74         exit (8);
75     }
76
77     sum();
78
79     return(0);
80 }
```

(Next Hint 350. Answer 114.)

PART II
HINTS

Hint 1: During the early days of the railroads, they had a problem with trains hitting each other where the tracks crossed. So they passed a law:

> When two trains approach each other at a place where the rails cross, both shall stop and remain stopped until the other one has proceeded it.

(Answer 24.)

Hint 2: UNIX uses `<line-feed>` to end lines. Microsoft Windows uses `<carriage-return><line-feed>`. (Answer 5.)

Hint 3: The statement:

```
if (n2 =! 0)
```

is not doing its job unless its job is to confuse you, in which case it's doing an excellent job. (Next Hint 82. Answer 25.)

Hint 4: The constructor does a proper job of initializing the magic numbers. Or it would if it were called. But everyone knows there is no way to create a variable without calling the constructor. Well, almost everyone. (Next Hint 300. Answer 98.)

Hint 5: What's the difference between simple macros and parameterized macros? (Answer 113.)

Hint 6: Operating system calls are expensive. (Answer 96.)

Hint 7: `unsigned char privs`

(Next Hint 313. Answer 11.)

Hint 8: Tree surgeon's law: Don't cut off the limb on which you are standing. (Next Hint 317. Answer 75.)

Hint 9: The program does not fail on complex instruction set machines such as the 80x86 CPUs, but fails on RISC machines such as Sparcs. It also fails on the Celerity 1000[3], which is where I found the problem. (Next Hint 143. Answer 52.)

Hint 10: This program reads data one character at a time. It's supposed to write data one character at a time. (Next Hint 102. Answer 99.)

Hint 11: When the programmer tries to set the `debugging` variable, he gets the error message:

```
debugging -- no such variable or class
```

(Next Hint 105. Answer 84.)

Hint 12: Check the preprocessor output. (Answer 82.)

---

[3] The Celerity 1000 was one of the first RISC minicomputers. Unfortunately the company that created it is no longer in business.

Hint 13: The g++ compiler issues the warnings:

```
var.cpp: In function `int main()':
var.cpp:14: warning: unused variable `bool remove'
var.cpp:16: warning: the address of `int remove(const char*)', will always be
    `true'
```

(Answer 35.)

Hint 14: The optimizer feels free to play games with your code. (Answer 114.)

Hint 15: The results are system-dependent. (Next Hint 278. Answer 63.)

Hint 16: M_PI is correct, but the wrong result is printed. (Next Hint 170. Answer 10.)

Hint 17: The comma operator returns the result of the second expression. So the expression 5,9 has the value 9. (Next Hint 348. Answer 86.)

Hint 18: You can't. (Next Hint 344. Answer 80.)

Hint 19: The printf function gets lost and starts making things up. (Next Hint 31. Answer 85.)

Hint 20: The number of times the body of the loop is executed is probably smaller thank you think. (Next Hint 36. Answer 89.)

Hint 21: If you're using MS-DOS, the result depends on the memory model. (Next Hint 130. Answer 21.)

Hint 22: Failure is system-dependent. (Next Hint 9. Answer 52.)

Hint 23: When is the destructor for true_name called? When is the string used? (Answer 30.)

Hint 24: The more functions you call between the call to tmp_name and where you use the results, the more likely you will get a bad result. (Next Hint 85. Answer 18.)

Hint 25: C++ is only partially typesafe. (Next Hint 63. Answer 7.)

Hint 26: Static data is dangerous. (Answer 100.)

Hint 27: Resources required: resource1, resource2 – or is that resource2, resource1? (Next Hint 1. Answer 24.)

Hint 28: Run the program through the preprocessor. (Next Hint 327. Answer 29.)

Hint 29: How many times is the loop executed? (Next Hint 20. Answer 89.)

Hint 30: Borland compilers let you define at compile time if the default for character variables is signed or unsigned. (Next Hint 60. Answer 8.)

Hint 31: C does not do parameter checking of printf calls. (Next Hint 277. Answer 85.)

Hint 32: The answer depends on who wrote your heap management library. (Answer 77.)

Hint 33: Run the program through the preprocessor and look at the result. (Next Hint 179. Answer 105.)

Hint 34: The results are:

```
11072   12627   16262
3157    3664    5034
13605   16307   22366
```

(Next Hint 158. Answer 53.)

Hint 35: Preprocessor syntax is not C++ syntax. (Next Hint 284. Answer 82.)

Hint 36: What do we do with result after we compute it? (Next Hint 152. Answer 89.)

Hint 37: Anyone who would program i++++ should be shot. (Next Hint 272. Answer 87.)

Hint 38: The statement:

```
counter == 10;
```

is a valid C++ statement. It doesn't do anything, but it's valid. (Next Hint 205. Answer 112.)

Hint 39: Can you express 1/3 as a decimal number exactly? Can the computer express 0.1 as a floating-point number exactly? (The answer is the same for both.) (Answer 107.)

Hint 40: The problem is on an earlier line, not line 16. (Next Hint 346. Answer 79.)

Hint 41: height never gets assigned 2. (Next Hint 78. Answer 62.)

Hint 42: The dictionary file is in alphabetical order. (Next Hint 311. Answer 74.)

Hint 43: What does an_array.operator = (an_array) do? (Answer 75.)

Hint 44: Indentation is incorrect. (Next Hint 156. Answer 31.)

Hint 45: The g++ compiler outputs the warning:

```
semi.cpp: In function `int main()':
semi.cpp:15: warning: statement with no effect
```

(Next Hint 35. Answer 82.)

Hint 46: What you see is what you get — literally. (Next Hint 307. Answer 69.)

Hint 47: The output is:

```
One million 1
```

(Next Hint 59. Answer 44.)

Hint 48: What happens to the buffer at the end of the function call? (Answer 83.)

Hint 49: The compiler can decide execution order for some multipart statements. (Answer 26.)

Hint 50: This program generates no compiler warning. (Next Hint 318. Answer 20.)

Hint 51: Two problems are related to what is put in struct data. (I know that makes four, but one falls into both categories.) (Answer 71.)

Hint 52: You know what this hint should be, don't you? (Next Hint 207. Answer 42.)

Hint 53: We have two functions that are calling each result in an infinite recursion. Because there are only three member functions, it should not be too hard to figure out which ones are causing the problem. (Next Hint 125. Answer 12.)

Hint 54: Operator precedence. (Answer 49.)

Hint 55: I didn't know that you could put commas in C++ numbers. (Next Hint 335. Answer 44.)

Hint 56: Where's delete called? (Answer 32.)

Hint 57: Double precision is 64 bits. The C standard is to have all floating-point done in double.

All this has nothing to do with the problem. (Incidentally, getting a 64-bit fraction out of a 64-bit floating-point format is a neat trick.) (Next Hint 94. Answer 73.)

Hint 58: 0d is the ASCII for carriage return. (Next Hint 234. Answer 5.)

Hint 59: The g++ compiler issues the warning:

```
comma.cpp: In function `int main()':
comma.cpp:12: warning: left-hand operand of comma expression has no effect
```

(Next Hint 126. Answer 44.)

Hint 60: The g++ compiler issues the warning:

```
chff.cpp: In function `int main()':
chff.cpp:13: warning: comparison is always 0 due to limited range of data type
```

(Answer 8.)

Hint 61: The uncaught exception is of class problem. Honest! (Next Hint 339. Answer 55.)

Hint 62: The character "A" has the integer value 65. The integer value of "A"+1 is 66. This is related to the output:

```
A6667
```

(Answer 45.)

Hint 63: Externs are not typesafe in C++. (Answer 7.)

Hint 64: The `fork` system call creates a duplicate process with duplicate memory. (Next Hint 252. Answer 50.)

Hint 65: The program dumps core. (Next Hint 282. Answer 115.)

Hint 66: The indentation is off. (Answer 97.)

Hint 67: Don't count on the indentation being correct. (Answer 13.)

Hint 68: What is the exit code returned to the operating system by this program? (Answer 6.)

Hint 69: Results are system-dependent. (Next Hint 279. Answer 94.)

Hint 70: Some sample runs:

```
Enter two integers: 100 3
Result is: 100


Enter two integers: 37 0
Result is: 37
```

(Next Hint 3. Answer 25.)

Hint 71: The `\n` character shows up where it's not wanted. (Answer 33.)

Hint 72: The C++ strings handle everything for us. But there's one thing they do behind our back that causes trouble. (Next Hint 162. Answer 36.)

Hint 73: The program dumps core when run. (Next Hint 182. Answer 95.)

Hint 74: On most systems the command:

```
$ program
```

will work, and the command:

```
$ program >output.txt
```

will fail. (Next Hint 197. Answer 83.)

Hint 75: What type of parameter is `out_file`? (Next Hint 159. Answer 40.)

Hint 76: In binary, 3 is 0011. In binary, 12 is 1100. (Next Hint 218. Answer 17.)

Hint 77: The error occurs when the open fails. (Next Hint 288. Answer 60.)

Hint 78: The statement

```
11    height = 2;
```

is not an executable statement; it just looks like one. (Next Hint 287. Answer 62.)

Hint 79: When is `a_var` initialized and the constructor called? (Next Hint 137. Answer 111.)

Hint 80: Computers don't know basic mathematics. (Next Hint 268. Answer 1.)

Hint 81: No prototypes — no parameter checking. (Next Hint 174. Answer 41.)

Hint 82: The g++ compiler generates the warning:

```
not_z.cpp: In function `int main()':
not_z.cpp:13: warning: suggest parentheses around assignment used as truth
    value
```

(Next Hint 262. Answer 25.)

Hint 83: There is one variable declared for the two declarations. (Next Hint 148. Answer 57.)

Hint 84: What's `0x8000 >> 1`? (Answer 19.)

Hint 85: What's being pointed to? Who owns it? For how long? (Answer 18.)

Hint 86: Who owns the data being pointed to by each of the pointers. (Next Hint 26. Answer 100.)

Hint 87: Results are system-dependent. (Next Hint 21. Answer 21.)

Hint 88: Where is the data put for the statement:

```
printf("That's all\n");
```

(Next Hint 48. Answer 83.)

Hint 89: This is correct, legal, standard C++ even though it may not look like it to some people. (Next Hint 211. Answer 86.)

Hint 90: Run the output through the preprocessor. (Next Hint 273. Answer 88.)

Hint 91: The g++ compiler gives us a warning:

```
hbit.cpp: In function `void bit_out(short int)':
hbit.cpp:19: warning: overflow in implicit constant conversion
```

(Answer 2.)

Hint 92: It's obvious that the problem must be before line 28 because we don't see the `Starting....` message. (Next Hint 111. Answer 68.)

Hint 93: The output is:

```
i is 3
i is 2
```

(Answer 87.)

Hint 94: This is implementation-dependent. On some older systems, you get the proper number of bits accuracy. In general systems that emulate floating-point will report accurate results and systems with floating-point coprocessors will report exaggerated results. (Answer 73.)

Hint 95: The results are compile-time switch-dependent. (Next Hint 331. Answer 39.)

Hint 96: The gcc warnings are:

```
sum.c: In function `sum':
sum.c:13: warning: declaration of `i1' shadows a parameter
sum.c:14: warning: declaration of `i2' shadows a parameter
sum.c:15: warning: declaration of `i3' shadows a parameter
```

(Answer 94.)

Hint 97: Race condition. Ties cause a dead stop. (Next Hint 27. Answer 24.)

Hint 98: remove is a flag. remove is not a flag. (Next Hint 221. Answer 35.)

Hint 99: Humans print the zip code for Boston as 02126. C++ sees things differently. (Next Hint 308. Answer 15.)

Hint 100: Sample output:

```
Area of sample is 0
```

(Next Hint 326. Answer 93.)

Hint 101: This was an old C program ported to C++ by an old C programmer. (Next Hint 120. Answer 98.)

Hint 102: The output looks something like:

```
4742106811710132116111321151111091013298114971051
010097109971031011003211211411110311497109321141
01
1131171051141011091011101161154410116104101321021
1
...
```

(Next Hint 160. Answer 99.)

Hint 103: Results are system-dependent. (Next Hint 314. Answer 90.)

Hint 104: On a MS-DOS system, the Cleveland zip code is a negative number. (Next Hint 223. Answer 104.)

Hint 105: The optimizer can do a lot of work on this code. (Answer 84.)

Hint 106: The g++ compiler issues the warning:

```
comment.cpp:19:35: warning: "/*" within comment
```

(Answer 91.)

Hint 107: The results are compile-time switch-dependent. (Next Hint 29. Answer 89.)

Hint 108: What is a buffer? (Next Hint 263. Answer 68.)

Hint 109: What do setjmp and longjmp *not* do? (Answer 66.)

Hint 110: An exception is not being caught. At first glance, this may seem impossible because there is only one exception class, problem, which we catch. Even if we didn't catch it, the catch(...) should catch everything else. (Next Hint 173. Answer 55.)

Hint 111: Nothing is obvious in programming. (Answer 68.)

Hint 112: It's an off by one error. (Next Hint 227. Answer 38.)

Hint 113: Write 1/3 in decimal. (Next Hint 302. Answer 54.)

Hint 114: It's always the same number each time. (Next Hint 66. Answer 97.)

Hint 115: Two ifs, one else. So which if does the else belong to? (Answer 31.)

Hint 116: The result is system-dependent. You may be lucky and get the right answer, or you may get random numbers. (Answer 51.)

Hint 117: What's the range of a short int? (Answer 1.)

Hint 118: Funny macro definition. (Next Hint 190. Answer 113.)

Hint 119: The bombing is compiler-dependent. On the cheap compilers you get a core dump. The better ones print an error message telling you that you called a pure virtual function. (Next Hint 237. Answer 101.)

Hint 120: There's no way to change a constant in a class. Yet if we run this through the debugger we find that the magic numbers are 0 instead of their intended values. (Next Hint 4. Answer 98.)

Hint 121: The problem is compilation flag-dependent. (Next Hint 14. Answer 114.)

Hint 122: The output is:

```
11 squared is 121
```

not the squares of 1 to 10 as the programmer expected. (Answer 34.)

Hint 123: The item printed is not an integer. (Next Hint 149. Answer 86.)

Hint 124: The variable ch is a character. What is ch+1? (Next Hint 283. Answer 45.)

Hint 125: Count the number of times the copy constructor is called. (Next Hint 235. Answer 12.)

Hint 126: "000" is a legal C++ statement. Totally useless, but legal. (Answer 44.)

Hint 127: Yes, buffered I/O is useful to a program like this. But not the way it's done here even though we're using the buffered I/O library *iostream*. (Answer 65.)

Hint 128: How many times is the multiply being done? (Answer 39.)

Hint 129: The results can depend on what compiler flags are used at compile time. (Next Hint 310. Answer 9.)

Hint 130: Intel machines have a very brain-damaged segmented pointer architecture. (Next Hint 231. Answer 21.)

Hint 131: Results are compiler-dependent. (Next Hint 141. Answer 8.)

Hint 132: A process switch can occur at any time. (Next Hint 276. Answer 92.)

Hint 133: The preprocessor is not C++. (Next Hint 360. Answer 46.)

Hint 134: Here's one method:

```
if (i == 2)
    i = 1;
else
    i = 2;
```

But there's a faster method. (Next Hint 140. Answer 48.)

Hint 135: The answer is system-dependent. (Next Hint 264. Answer 70.)

Hint 136: Octal. (Answer 15.)

Hint 137: When is std::cout initialized? (Answer 111.)

Hint 138: g++ warning:

```
comment.cpp:11: warning: `/*' within comment
```
(Answer 62.)

Hint 139: I expected the program to print:

```
First 1
First 1
First 1
Second 1
Second 2
Second 3
```

This is not what was printed. (Next Hint 297. Answer 102.)

Hint 140: Here's another method:

```
i = (i == 2) ? 1 : 2;
```

But there's a faster method. (Next Hint 216. Answer 48.)

Hint 141: Results can be changed by compile-time switches on some compilers. (Next Hint 30. Answer 8.)

Hint 142: Constructors for a derived class are called in the order "base, derived." Destructors are called in the order "derived, base." (Answer 101.)

Hint 143: The statement:

```
flags |= CD_SIGNAL;
```

is supposed to set a single bit in flags. Most of the time it does so. (Answer 52.)

Hint 144: The output is:

```
----------------
```

(Next Hint 91. Answer 2.)

Hint 145: What is the type of variable being passed in? What is the parameter type as far as the function is concerned? (Next Hint 315. Answer 72.)

Hint 146: The C++ `std::string` class allocates memory. But it also destroys it and is carefully designed to avoid memory leaks. (Next Hint 359. Answer 66.)

Hint 147: Some compilers, including the one used for this program, let you optimize and debug. (Next Hint 11. Answer 84.)

Hint 148: The g++ issues the warning:

```
/tmp/cckuUagE.o: In function `std::string::_M_data() const':
/home/sdo/local/include/g++-v3/i586-pc-linux-gnu/bits/gthr-
single.h(.data+0x0): multiple definition of `value'
/tmp/ccenmAbd.o(.data+0x0):/home/sdo/local/include/g++-v3/i586-pc-linux-gnu/
bits/gthr-single.h: first defined here
collect2: ld returned 1 exit status
```

(Answer 57.)

Hint 149: The item printed is a pointer. (Next Hint 347. Answer 86.)

Hint 150: When does the string `first_name` get initialized? When does `full_name`? Who enforces that order? (Answer 3.)

Hint 151: `'\n'` is newline. (Answer 37.)

Hint 152: If we do nothing with `result`, then why bother to compute it? (Answer 89.)

Hint 153: The declaration

```
struct info *new_info(void)
```

contains a clue.(Next Hint 101. Answer 98.)

Hint 154: How many pointers are there? How many things are they pointing to? (Next Hint 209. Answer 64.)

Hint 155: The g++ compiler outputs the warning:

```
equal.cpp: In function `int main()':
equal.cpp:15: warning: suggest parentheses around assignment used as truth value
```

(Next Hint 208. Answer 47.)

Hint 156: Output is:

```
Customer must pay -10
```

(Next Hint 115. Answer 31.)

Hint 157: Your results may vary. (Next Hint 79. Answer 111.)

Hint 158: SAIL and C share almost no syntax. The two languages are entirely different. Yet the same single-character mistake is responsible for both programs going wrong. (Next Hint 220. Answer 53.)

Hint 159: Normally C++ uses "pass by value" to pass parameters. That means that the value is copied into the subroutine. (Next Hint 233. Answer 40.)

Hint 160: The output contains a bunch of integers. (Answer 99.)

Hint 161: I count 3. (Next Hint 293. Answer 71.)

Hint 162: This looks a lot like Program 58. (Next Hint 178. Answer 36.)

Hint 163: What does ++i return? What does i++ return? (Next Hint 93. Answer 87.)

Hint 164: Your results may vary. (Next Hint 19. Answer 85.)

Hint 165: Everyone knows that (x*4)/4 = x. That is basic mathematics. (Next Hint 80. Answer 1.)

Hint 166: If you think the compile time switches have to do with optimization, you're wrong. (Next Hint 358. Answer 63.)

Hint 167: What numbers can be represented by a 3-bit signed number? (Next Hint 169. Answer 42.)

Hint 168: The output is:

```
Division 5
```

(Next Hint 202. Answer 91.)

Hint 169: What numbers can be represented by a 2-bit signed number? (Next Hint 52. Answer 42.)

Hint 170: What's printed is:

```
pi is 1413754136
```

Results are machine-dependent. (Next Hint 203. Answer 10.)

Hint 171: All bit arrays are not the same size. (Next Hint 353. Answer 56.)

Hint 172: What you see is what you get. (Next Hint 46. Answer 69.)

Hint 173: So where does the uncaught exception come from? (Next Hint 61. Answer 55.)

Hint 174: gcc produced the warnings:

```
strcat.c: In function `full_name':
strcat.c:19: warning: implicit declaration of function `strcpy'
strcat.c:20: warning: implicit declaration of function `strcat'
strcat.c:20: warning: passing arg 2 of `strcat' makes pointer from integer witho
ut a cast
strcat.c: In function `main':
strcat.c:28: warning: implicit declaration of function `printf'
```

(Answer 41.)

Hint 175: The statement is absolutely useless if the program is run normally. (Next Hint 232. Answer 80.)

Hint 176: Your results may vary. (Next Hint 24. Answer 18.)

Hint 177: Results are system- and compiler-dependent. (Next Hint 49. Answer 26.)

Hint 178: This is a C++ version of the error in Program 58. (Answer 36.)

Hint 179: The `ABORT` statement looks like a statement. It's not. (Answer 105.)

Hint 180: The output is:

```
-XXXXXXXXXXXXXXX
```

(Next Hint 303. Answer 19.)

Hint 181: Where does `scanf` leave the file when it stops reading? (Answer 28.)

Hint 182: The program dumps core when doing the `sscanf`. (Next Hint 254. Answer 95.)

Hint 183: Is buffered I/O useful in this case? (Next Hint 213. Answer 65.)

Hint 184: The problem involves the overuse of `delete`. (Next Hint 188. Answer 115.)

Hint 185: We don't always close the file after opening it. The result is that we run out of file descriptors. We need to add some `close(fd)` statements. (That's 2 of the 3 problems.) (Answer 60.)

Hint 186: The program uses `inline` with functions that someone points to. Can that be part of the problem? (Next Hint 219. Answer 77.)

Hint 187: There's what looks like a useless semicolon at the end of:

```
result=result/*divisor;   /* Do divide */;
```

It's not useless. (Next Hint 245. Answer 91.)

Hint 188: The operator `delete` is used in the copy constructor. What's being deleted? (Answer 115.)

Hint 189: How many instances of the `an_array` variable are there? (Next Hint 329. Answer 59.)

Hint 190: Run it through the preprocessor. (Next Hint 5. Answer 113.)

Hint 191: What is being returned? (Next Hint 23. Answer 30.)

Hint 192: The output is system-dependent. (Next Hint 90. Answer 88.)

Hint 193: The indentation is not correct. (Next Hint 122. Answer 34.)

Hint 194: The results are system-dependent. (Next Hint 324. Answer 112.)

Hint 195: `prev_ch` is created a lot. (Answer 106.)

Hint 196: What's modified by `volatile`? (Answer 61.)

Hint 197: The `setbuf` causes the data to be put where? (Next Hint 88. Answer 83.)

Hint 198: `M_PI` is defined in *math.h* as

```
#define M_PI 3.14159265358979323846 /* pi */
```

(Next Hint 16. Answer 10.)

Hint 199: What does the function:

```
trouble operator = (const trouble &i_trouble)
```

return? (Next Hint 333. Answer 109.)

Hint 200: It does not print what's expected. (Next Hint 192. Answer 88.)

Hint 201: Output:

```
The area is 367
```

(Next Hint 259. Answer 29.)

Hint 202: So why does the division not happen? (Next Hint 187. Answer 91.)

Hint 203: The g++ compiler reports the warnings:

```
pi.c: In function `main':
pi.c:12: warning: int format, double arg (arg 2)
```

(Answer 10.)

Hint 204: The output is:

```
Y=8
```

(Next Hint 54. Answer 49.)

Hint 205: MAX is not 10. (Answer 112.)

Hint 206: The printing is correct as far as C++ is concerned. (Next Hint 99. Answer 15.)

Hint 207: The g++ compiler issues the warning:

```
bit.cpp: In function `int main()':
bit.cpp:33: warning: comparison is always 0 due to width of bitfield
```

(Answer 42.)

Hint 208: Typical runs:

```
$ equal
Enter current balance: 10
You owe 0
$ equal
Enter current balance: 0
You owe 0
$ equal
Enter current balance: -10
You owe 0
```

(Next Hint 267. Answer 47.)

Hint 209: There is only one name variable and two pointers. (Answer 64.)

Hint 210: In what order are the constant members initialized? (Next Hint 100. Answer 93.)

Hint 211: The results are system-dependent. (Next Hint 123. Answer 86.)

Hint 212: Results are system-dependent. (Next Hint 225. Answer 110.)

Hint 213: Is buffered I/O used in this case? (Next Hint 127. Answer 65.)

Hint 214: Obviously, it prints Hello once and two new lines. But it is equally obvious it wouldn't be in this book if it did the sane thing. (Next Hint 64. Answer 50.)

Hint 215: It looks like there is a comment on line 10 and a comment on line 11. That's not quite right. There's a comment on lines 10 and 11. (Next Hint 138. Answer 62.)

Hint 216: The fastest method uses no comparison and one subtraction. (Answer 48.)

Hint 217: The program outputs:

```
Error: Could not open
oot
ewable
```

(Next Hint 243. Answer 37.)

Hint 218: "Bitwise And" is not "Logical And". (Answer 17.)

Hint 219: The program uses inline with functions that someone points to. Can that be part of the problem? No. That has nothing to do with it. C++ handles this situation just fine. (Next Hint 271. Answer 77.)

Hint 220: If this were a cipher a frequency analysis of the numbers might provide a clue. Actually this is not a cipher, but a frequency analysis of the digits can prove interesting. (Next Hint 341. Answer 53.)

Hint 221: remove is two things. (Next Hint 13. Answer 35.)

Hint 222: Race condition. (Next Hint 132. Answer 92.)

Hint 223: Most UNIX compilers use 32 bits for an integer. On MS-DOS (and I mean MS-DOS, not Microsoft Windows), integers are usually 16 bits. (Next Hint 258. Answer 104.)

Hint 224: Typical run:

```
% calc
Enter operator and value:+ 5
Total: 5
Enter operator and value:+ 10
Bad operator entered
Total: 5
Enter operator and value:Bad operator entered
Total: 5
Enter operator and value:q
Bad operator entered
```

```
Total: 5
Enter operator and value:q
```

(Next Hint 257. Answer 28.)

Hint 225: What do you think it takes to get the log_file initialized? (Answer 110.)

Hint 226: There are no less than three errors in this program, all of a similar nature. (Next Hint 77. Answer 60.)

Hint 227: What happens if the balance is 0. (Answer 38.)

Hint 228: This program compiles and works on all the known C++ compilers. Yet it is wrong! How can that be? (Next Hint 321. Answer 6.)

Hint 229: The byte after 09 is wrong. (Next Hint 58. Answer 5.)

Hint 230: Alignment and padding. (Next Hint 249. Answer 103.)

Hint 231: On Intel machines, in some memory models, the compiler generates code to manipulate only the address part of a pointer and leaves the segment alone. (Answer 21.)

Hint 232: The statement is useful only if you run the program in an interactive debugger. (Next Hint 309. Answer 81.)

Hint 233: What does it mean to copy an ostream variable? (Answer 40.)

Hint 234: 0a is the ASCII for line feed. (Next Hint 2. Answer 5.)

Hint 235: The copy constructor is called in two places. (Answer 12.)

Hint 236: How many times is var_array::~var_array called? (Next Hint 286. Answer 59.)

Hint 237: The compiler works very hard to keep you from calling a pure virtual function. You can't declare an instance of an abstract class, and any base class must have a derived version that defines all the pure virtual functions. That means that any pure virtual function will have a real definition in the base class.

So how did we manage to call one if we know that there must be an implementation of the virtual function in the derived class? (Next Hint 142. Answer 101.)

Hint 238: Common sense tells you that if you declare an array as

```
int array[5]
```

then the elements are:

```
array[1], array[2], array[3], array[4], array[5]
```

Common sense has nothing to do with programming. (Answer 90.)

Hint 239: The following is a hex dump of the MS-DOS output:

```
000000 00 01 02 03 04 05 06 07 08 09 0d 0a 0b 0c 0d 0e
000010 0f 10 11 12 13 14 15 16 17 18 19 1a 1b 1c 1d 1e
000020 1f 20 21 22 23 24 25 26 27 28 29 2a 2b 2c 2d 2e
000030 2f 30 31 32 33 34 35 36 37 38 39 3a 3b 3c 3d 3e
000040 3f 40 41 42 43 44 45 46 47 48 49 4a 4b 4c 4d 4e
000050 4f 50 51 52 53 54 55 56 57 58 59 5a 5b 5c 5d 5e
000060 5f 60 61 62 63 64 65 66 67 68 69 6a 6b 6c 6d 6e
000070 6f 70 71 72 73 74 75 76 77 78 79 7a 7b 7c 7d 7e
000080 7f
```

(Next Hint 229. Answer 5.)

Hint 240: Comma is a C++ operator. (Next Hint 47. Answer 44.)

Hint 241: Thread switching can occur between any two lines like these two:

```
++count;   // We've got a new character
*in_ptr = ch;// Store the character
```

(Answer 92.)

Hint 242: The g++ compiler reports the warning:

```
def.cpp: In function `int main()':
def.cpp:19: warning: label `defualt' defined but not used
```

(Answer 67.)

Hint 243: On UNIX, name is 15 characters long. On MS-DOS, it's only 12 characters long. (Next Hint 151. Answer 37.)

Hint 244: Using g++ when the program is compiled.

```
g++ -g -Wall -o last last.cpp first.cpp
```

it works. But when compiled as:

```
g++ -g -Wall -o last first.cpp last.cpp
```

it fails.
(Next Hint 150. Answer 3.)

Hint 245: If you have syntax highlighting in your editor, see what happens when you put this code into it. (Next Hint 338. Answer 91.)

Hint 246: It's obvious that the answer is 3. (i++ is 2 and one more ++ makes 3.) But nothing's obvious in programming. (Next Hint 37. Answer 87.)

Hint 247: Spacing. (Next Hint 325. Answer 23.)

Hint 248: There are two variable declarations in this program. (Next Hint 83. Answer 57.)

Hint 249: 6 is not divisible by 4. (Answer 103.)

Hint 250: The redefined new function should work because it's obvious that all bit arrays are the same size. (Next Hint 171. Answer 56.)

Hint 251: Watch your end. (Answer 43.)

Hint 252: The fork system call creates a duplicate process with duplicate memory, and that includes printf data that has been buffered. (Answer 50.)

Hint 253: Normal people count five things by saying, "1, 2, 3, 4, 5." C++ programmers say, "0, 1, 2, 3, 4." (Next Hint 238. Answer 90.)

Hint 254: gcc warnings:

```
calc2.c: In function `main':
calc2.c:24: warning: format argument is not a pointer (arg 3)
calc2.c:24: warning: format argument is not a pointer (arg 4)
```

(Answer 95.)

Hint 255: The preprocessor does not understand C++ syntax. (Next Hint 295. Answer 78.)

Hint 256: The problem usually goes away if you try to debug the program. (Next Hint 121. Answer 114.)

Hint 257: Your results may vary. (Next Hint 181. Answer 28.)

Hint 258: A 16-bit integer can go from 32767 to -32768. (Answer 104.)

Hint 259: The result is 367 (330 + 37). (Answer 29.)

Hint 260: strcmp does not return true/false. (Answer 76.)

Hint 261: char prev_ch = '\0'; is executed when prev_ch is created. (Next Hint 195. Answer 106.)

Hint 262: The statement

```
if (n2 =! 0)
```

change n2. (Answer 25.)

Hint 263: The UNIX designers in their infinite wisdom issue the message:

```
Floating exception (core dumped)
```

for an integer divide by zero. (Next Hint 92. Answer 68.)

Hint 264: Some systems let you dereference NULL; others do not. (Answer 70.)

Hint 265: Not in this book! (Next Hint 72. Answer 36.)

Hint 266: The expression x << 2 is really 4. However, we don't use this expression in this program. (Next Hint 204. Answer 49.)

Hint 267: The statement:

```
if (amount = 0)
```

does not compare 0 and amount. (Answer 47.)

Hint 268: The output of this program is:

```
The number of sheep is: 100
The number of sheep is: 1000
The number of sheep is: -6384
```

(Next Hint 117. Answer 1.)

Hint 269: char * != char[] (Next Hint 25. Answer 7.)

Hint 270: The output is:

```
Size is 25
```

not

```
Size is 20
```

as the programmer expected. (Answer 4.)

Hint 271: The answer is system-dependent. (Next Hint 32. Answer 77.)

Hint 272: Should it be infeasible to shoot him or her, the person should be enlightened as to what good programming style is. (Next Hint 163. Answer 87.)

Hint 273: The output on one system looks like:

```
3 squared is 9
5 squared is 25
7 squared is 49
9 squared is 81
11 squared is 121
```

(Answer 88.)

Hint 274: The switch statement does not have a default case; it just looks like it. (Next Hint 242. Answer 67.)

Hint 275: There's nothing wrong with line 16. We asked about it to fool you. (Next Hint 40. Answer 79.)

Hint 276: The reader performs these two lines:

```
++count;    // We've got a new character
*in_ptr = ch;// Store the character
```

(Next Hint 241. Answer 92.)

Hint 277: gcc warning:

```
two.c: In function `main':
two.c:11: warning: too few arguments for format
two.c:9: warning: unused variable `answer'
```

(Answer 85.)

Hint 278: Some compilers have a switch that will change the behavior of the program. The switch won't fix things, but the program will act differently. (Next Hint 166. Answer 63.)

Hint 279: There's more than one i1. (Next Hint 96. Answer 94.)

Hint 280: Know the difference between "and" and "and and". (Next Hint 76. Answer 17.)

Hint 281: The program prints:

```
Result is 0
```

(Answer 27.)

Hint 282: If you examine the code, I always make sure to delete the variable data before I overwrite it. (Next Hint 184. Answer 115.)

Hint 283: The output is:

```
A6667
```

(Next Hint 62. Answer 45.)

Hint 284: The statement:

```
-1.0;
```

is a good C++ statement. Although totally useless, the statement is perfectly legal. (Next Hint 12. Answer 82.)

Hint 285: Because there are no headers, we have no prototypes for the standard functions; they are declared implicitly. (Next Hint 81. Answer 41.)

Hint 286: var_array::~var_array is called twice. (Answer 59.)

Hint 287: If you have an editor with syntax coloring, it will display base in one color and height in another. (Next Hint 215. Answer 62.)

Hint 288: The open fails even when the file is present and the permissions allow the reading of the file. (Next Hint 306. Answer 60.)

Hint 289: The statement

```
int &i = 3+4;
```

is illegal. But don't worry; we don't use it – at least not in this form. (Answer 22.)

Hint 290: The output is:

```
Width is too small
area(10, 10) = 100
```

What the programmer expected is:

```
Width is too small
area(10, 50) = 500
```

(Next Hint 67. Answer 13.)

Hint 291: The copy constructor is called more than you might think. (Next Hint 316. Answer 109.)

Hint 292: Remember "1" is not the same as "1.0". (Next Hint 281. Answer 27.)

Hint 293: Two problems involve the number of bytes in struct data. (Next Hint 51. Answer 71.)

Hint 294: strcmp can confuse a novice. (Next Hint 260. Answer 76.)

Hint 295: Run the output through the preprocessor. (Answer 78.)

Hint 296: Sample output:

```
Stack 0 has 1 elements
Stack 1 has 100 elements
Stack 2 has 134516168 elements
Stack 3 has 134525376 elements
Stack 4 has 4 elements
```

(Next Hint 145. Answer 72.)

Hint 297: What is the value of i++? What is the value of ++i? (Answer 102.)

Hint 298: They're different. (Next Hint 255. Answer 78.)

Hint 299: The numbers appear to be octal. (Answer 53.)

Hint 300: It's impossible to change a constant inside a class, yet this program does. It's impossible to create a class without calling the constructor, yet this program does. (Answer 98.)

Hint 301: This program prints:

```
parity
-break
xon
-rts
```

(Answer 108.)

Hint 302: Write 1/3 in decimal three times in a column. Now add them up. (Answer 54.)

Hint 303: 0x8000 (1000 0000 0000(b)) is (1<<15). That's the correct value and what the programmer expected. (Next Hint 84. Answer 19.)

Hint 304: Indentation is incorrect. (Next Hint 270. Answer 4.)

Hint 305: Making your own new function can speed up things greatly — if you do it right. (Next Hint 250. Answer 56.)

Hint 306: The open fails with an EMFILE error. (The process already has the maximum number of files open.) (Next Hint 185. Answer 60.)

Hint 307: The string:

```
"Hello World!/n"
```

contains 14 characters. (Answer 69.)

Hint 308: The program prints

```
San Diego 92126
Boston    01110
```

(Next Hint 136. Answer 15.)

Hint 309: The programmer thinks that something funny is happening when data item #500 is read. (Answer 81.)

Hint 310: How many times is *in_port_ptr read? (Next Hint 356. Answer 9.)

Hint 311: The data structure used is an unbalanced binary tree. (Next Hint 323. Answer 74.)

Hint 312: I didn't know you could do triple comparisons like a<b<c. (Next Hint 18. Answer 80.)

Hint 313: A character has 8 bits. What are their numbers? (Answer 11.)

Hint 314: Sometimes when you run the program you get the wrong answer, sometimes you dump core with a segmentation violation (Windows users will get a UAE – Unexpected Application Error), and sometimes things work just fine. (Next Hint 253. Answer 90.)

Hint 315: What's the size of the element of the arrays? (Answer 72.)

```
sizeof(stack) != sizeof(safe_stack)
```

Hint 316: Sample output:

```
Copy Constructor called
= operator called
Copy Constructor called
- operator called
Copy Constructor called
= operator called

...
```

(Next Hint 199. Answer 109.)

Hint 317: This program tries to copy data just after it deletes it. (Next Hint 43. Answer 75.)

Hint 318: What are the arguments to memset? (Next Hint 337. Answer 20.)

Hint 319: Results are system-dependent. (Next Hint 191. Answer 30.)

Hint 320: There's a reason that we didn't include any headers in this program. (Next Hint 285. Answer 41.)

Hint 321: The program is nonstandard. (Next Hint 68. Answer 6.)

Hint 322: Hey, isn't this the program we just did in Program 58? No, actually it's the program you just did with a fix applied. Notice the nice **static** declaration on line 22. (But it's still got problems.) (Next Hint 154. Answer 64.)

Hint 323: The data structure used is a *very* unbalanced binary tree. (Answer 74.)

Hint 324: Check the preprocessor output. (Next Hint 38. Answer 112.)

Hint 325: This program needs "blank", "blank", and "blank". (Answer 23.)

Hint 326: The g++ compiler reports the warning:

```
rect.cpp: In constructor `rectangle::rectangle(int, int)':
rect.cpp:20: warning: member initializers for `const int rectangle::height'
rect.cpp:18: warning:   and `const int rectangle::area'
rect.cpp:31: warning:   will be re-ordered to match declaration order
```

(Answer 93.)

Hint 327: The preprocessor follows its own rules. (Next Hint 201. Answer 29.)

Hint 328: What is out_file? (Next Hint 75. Answer 40.)

Hint 329: There are two instances of the var_array class when store_it is executing. (Next Hint 355. Answer 59.)

Hint 330: When a function is not defined in the derived class, C++ will go to the base class for it.

So what stops C++ from calling base::print_it(int)? (Answer 58.)

Hint 331: We do store the result of the multiplication into result 1863 times. So the loop is being executed. (Next Hint 128. Answer 39.)

Hint 332: What's the number of the leftmost bit of a 16-bit word? (Next Hint 144. Answer 2.)

Hint 333: How does the operator = function return its result? (Answer 109.)

Hint 334: The assignment operator has a problem. (Next Hint 357. Answer 14.)

Hint 335: You can't. (Next Hint 240. Answer 44.)

Hint 336: There are things and pointers to things. (Next Hint 196. Answer 61.)

Hint 337: sizeof(array) is not a character and '\0' is not an integer. C++ is not smart enough to notice this. (Answer 20.)

Hint 338: Comments begin with /* and end with */. (Next Hint 106. Answer 91.)

Hint 339: It's the second time we throw the exception that is the problem. (Next Hint 345. Answer 55.)

Hint 340: There's more to a name than you may think. (Next Hint 71. Answer 33.)

Hint 341: If you did the frequency analysis, you would find that the digits 8 and 9 are missing from the output. (Next Hint 299. Answer 53.)

Hint 342: 12 * 34 = 408. It always is 408. Everyone knows this, including the compiler. (Answer 16.)

Hint 343: Alignment. (Next Hint 230. Answer 103.)

Hint 344: Why does the computer perform the test 1>c? (Answer 80.)

Hint 345: The second exception is thrown from the stack destructor. (Answer 55.)

Hint 346: The problem is on line 5. (Answer 79.)

Hint 347: The g++ compiler issues the warning:

```
array2.cpp: In function `int main()':
array2.cpp:17: warning: left-hand operand of comma expression has no effect
```

(Next Hint 17. Answer 86.)

Hint 348: matrix[2] is a pointer. (Answer 86.)

Hint 349: The MS-DOS version inserts one character. (Next Hint 239. Answer 5.)

Hint 350: The problem is compiler-dependent. (Next Hint 256. Answer 114.)

Hint 351: The program prints:

```
At least one number is zero.
```

(Next Hint 280. Answer 17.)

Hint 352: The program reports 64 bits of accuracy. (Next Hint 57. Answer 73.)

Hint 353: There's a reason the redefined new function is passed size as a parameter. (Answer 56.)

Hint 354: The program prints:

```
2 is prime
3 is prime
5 is prime
7 is prime
```

We expected a bunch of messages telling us that 4, 6, 8, and 9 are not prime. But for some reason those messages have disappeared. (Next Hint 274. Answer 67.)

Hint 355: How is the copy constructor implemented? (Next Hint 236. Answer 59.)

Hint 356: How many times does *in_port_ptr have to be read for the code to work? (At least on the surface level.) (Answer 9.)

Hint 357: What's being assigned by

```
save_queue = a_queue
```

(Answer 14.)

Hint 358: The compile-time switches have to do with how the conversion of `char` to `int` is handled. (Answer 63.)

Hint 359: What do `setjmp` and `longjmp` do? (Next Hint 109. Answer 66.)

Hint 360: Run it through the preprocessor. (Answer 46.)

Hint 361: Hey, Steve, can't you get this program right? (Next Hint 265. Answer 36.)

PART III
ANSWERS

Answer 1: The problem is that a large herd contains 10,000 sheep. That's 40,000 legs. The maximum number you can fit in a short int is 32,767. That's smaller than 40,000, so (10,000*4) causes an overflow that results in wrong data being output.

Answer 2: The problem is that the statement:

```
// The bit we are printing now
short int bit = (1<<16);
```

does not set the variable bit to 1000 0000 0000 0000(b). Instead, it sets it to 1 0000 0000 0000 0000(b). Unfortunately, it can't hold 17 bits, so the result is that it's set to zero.

Because it is zero, the bit test statement will always fail, giving use the result:

```
----------------
```

Answer 3: Global classes are initialized before main. Order is not guaranteed by the compiler. In particular, there is nothing to guarantee that first_name is initialized before it is used. So if the compiler chooses the wrong order, the program will output incorrect data or die.

Answer 4: The programmer thought he put two statements inside the if, but he forgot the curly braces.

So the statement:

```
if (size > MAX)
    std::cout << "Size is too large\n";
    size = MAX;
```

properly indented looks like:

```
if (size > MAX)
    std::cout << "Size is too large\n";
size = MAX;
```

What the programmer should have written is:

```
if (size > MAX)
{
    std::cout << "Size is too large\n";
    size = MAX;
}
```

Answer 5: The problem is that the file type was not specified as binary (ios::bin). The Microsoft Windows runtime library edits character output and inserts <carriage-return (0xD)> before each <line-feed (0xA)>. This explains the extra 0D in the file just before the 0A character.

Answer 6: The problem is the line:

```
6 void main()
```

The function `main` is not a `void` function. It's an `int`. The function returns an exit code to the operating system. A properly written "Hello World" looks like:

```
 1 /**********************************************
 2  * The "standard" hello world program.       *
 3  **********************************************/
 4 #include <ostream>
 5
 6 int main()
 7 {
 8     std::cout << "Hello world!\n";
 9     return (0);
10 }
```

When my wife first took programming, this was the first program she was taught (the void version). I changed the `void` to an `int` and she turned the paper in. The teaching assistant counted it wrong and changed it back.

Needless to say, I was not happy about this and wrote him a very snooty letter telling him that `main` was an `int` and quoting him chapter and verse of the C++ standard proving it. He wrote back and was extremely nice about the whole thing.

Answer 7: The problem is that *sub.cpp* defines `str` as a character array (`char []`). The extern statement in *main.cpp* defines `str` as a character *pointer* (`char *`).

Now character arrays and character pointers are interchangeable *almost* everywhere in C++. This is one of the few cases they are not. In this case, the program `main` thinks that `str` is a character pointer, so it goes to that location and reads the first four bytes expecting an address. The first four bytes are "Hell," which is not an address, and so the program crashes.

Avoidance 1: Always define externs in a header file. This header should always be included by the module where the item is defined and every module where it's used.

Answer 8: The problem is that `ch` can be a signed character. That means that if `ch` is `0xFF` when converted to a signed integer for comparison purposes you get `int(ch)=-1` (`0xFFFFFFFF`). That's not `0xFF` and the comparison fails.

Avoidance 2: Be careful when you use character variables to hold numbers. They may not do what you want them to.

Answer 9: The problem is that the optimizer looks at the code and sees that we read `*in_port_ptr` three times and then throws away the result. The optimizer then figures out that it can optimize the program and produce the same apparent results by taking out the lines 20, 21, and 22.

The solution is to declare the port pointers `volatile`. In Program 107 we've done this, but something is not quite right.

Answer 10: The answer is that the `printf` format (`%d`) does not match the parameter type (`double`). The programmer should have written:

```
12    printf("pi is %f\n", M_PI);
```

Answer 11: A character has 8 bits numbered 0 to 7. The bits can be represented by the constants $(1 << 0)$ to $(1 << 7)$.

There is no bit number 8, so the expression

```
privs |= P_BACKUP;    // P_BACKUP = (1 << 8)
```

does nothing because it sets a bit outside the boundary of the character. The result is that only the administration privilege is really set.

Answer 12: The `operator =` function call takes a single parameter of type `data_holder`. This type of parameter is a call by value parameter, so the copy constructor is called. The programmer making the copy constructor decided to take a shortcut and uses the `operator =` to implement the copy. So `operator =` calls the copy constructor, which calls `operator =` which calls the copy constructor . . . and so on until you run out of stack.

The `operator =` function should take a constant reference as its parameter type:

```
data_holder &operator = (
        const data_holder &old_data_holder) {
```

It should also return a reference to a data holder.

Avoidance 3: Use `const` references if possible when passing parameters. This avoids the extra cost of doing a copy of a call by value parameter.

Answer 13: The problem is with the `if` statement. In the first one:

```
if (width < MIN) {
    std::cout << "Width is too small\n";
    width = MIN;
```

the programmer forgot to put in the closing curly brace. That's OK; he made up for it by forgetting to put in an opening brace for the next if statement:

```
if (height < MIN)
    std::cout << "Height is too small\n";
    height = MIN;
}
```

If we properly indent the code, we can see the problem:

```
if (width < MIN) {
    std::cout << "Width is too small\n";
```

```
        width = MIN;

    if (height < MIN)
        std::cout << "Height is too small\n";
    height = MIN;
}
```

What the programmer should have written is:

```
if (width < MIN) {
    std::cout << "Width is too small\n";
    width = MIN;
}

if (height < MIN) {
    std::cout << "Height is too small\n";
    height = MIN;
}
```

Answer 14: The statement:

```
save_queue = a_queue
```

copies a queue of size 30 to a queue of size 20. In other words, the assignment operator (as implemented) allows us to copy different size queue. We should not be allowed to do this.

There are four ways to solve this problem:

1. Use the STL queue class.
2. Make the assignment operator private (and not allow any assignments).
3. Change the assignment operator so that it throws an exception if the size of the queue is not the same.
4. Change the queue class so that you can assign different size queues to each other.

Answer 15: The constant 02126 is octal because the leading digit is a zero. So in C++, 02126 (octal) is 1110 (decimal) and is not the zip code for Boston.

Answer 16: The problem is that the compiler knows what 12 * 34 equals, so instead of doing the multiply it optimizes the statement and turns it into:

```
18        result = 408;
```

Since the multiply is not done, the timing is off. Program 109 is an attempt to fix this problem.

Answer 17: The problem is that the programmer used bitwise and (&) instead of logical and (&&). A bitwise and of the two numbers gives us:

```
   3 0011
& 12 1100
=========
   0 0000
```

So the result is 0, the `if` clause is skipped, and the `else` clause is executed. Some programmers use the shorthand:

```
if (x)
```

for

```
if (x != 0)
```

(I discourage such shorthand.)

This is one example of why I don't like shortcuts. A better way of writing the `if` statement is:

```
if ((i1 != 0) && (i2 != 0))
```

Shortly after discovering this bug I told a colleague about it. I explained what happened and said, "I now know the difference between 'and' and 'and and'." I'm not sure what amazed me more, the fact that I came up with this sentence or the fact the he understood it.

Answer 18: The problem is that `tmp_name` returns a pointer to the local variable `name`. When the function ends, the storage for all nonstatic local variables is reclaimed. This includes the storage for `name`. Thus, the pointer returned points to a random, unallocated section of memory.

The next function call that comes along will probably clobber that storage and make `a_name` look really strange.

A solution to this problem is to declare `name` **static**.

(See Program 59 for a similar problem.)

Answer 19: The problem is that the statement

```
bit >>= 1;
```

does not move the bit over to the right one. Instead it does a "signed" shift, which copies the sign bit. Thus

```
0x8000 >> 1      1000 0000 0000 0000 (b)
```

is not

```
0x4000           0100 0000 0000 0000 (b)
```

as expected but instead

```
0xC000           1100 0000 0000 0000 (b)
```

Because of this problem, the bit testing gives incorrect results.

Answer 20: The arguments to `memset` are:

```
memset(
    void *ptr,// Pointer to the data
    int value,// Value to set
    size_t size// Number of bytes to fill
);
```

In this case, the value is `sizeof(array)` and the number of bytes to fill is 0. Since `size=0` nothing was done.

The programmer should have written:

```
memset(array, '\0', sizeof(array));
```

Answer 21: The C++ standard states that all pointers must point to the array or above. You can't point below the array.

In this example, we have an array on an Intel machine. The address of the array, in Intel strange pointer parlance, is:

```
5880:0000
```

The `data_ptr` variable starts out at:

```
5880:001E
```

It then gets decremented as long as it is greater than `data`. During its decrementation `data_ptr` goes to

```
5880:0000
```

That's equal to the address of the array data, so it's decremented again. (Remember that in this memory model, only the address part is changed.) The result is:

```
5880:FFFE
```

Now

```
data_ptr >= data
```

is evaluated. But `data_ptr` is now much greater than `data`, so the program continues.

The result is that the program writes over random data, which can cause the system to crash. But if it doesn't, `data_ptr` will go down to:

```
5880:0000
```

wrap, and the process will continue again.

Answer 22: The problem is that the function `max` returns a reference to a parameter. That parameter is `3+4`, which is an expression.

What C++ actually does when `min` is called is:

1. Creates a temporary (`tmp1`) and assigns it 1+2
2. Creates a temporary (`tmp2`) and assigns it 3+4

3. Calls `max(tmp1, tmp2)`

4. This function returns a reference to `tmp2`.

```
i = &tmp2
tmp1 destroyed
tmp2 destroyed
```

5. The variable `i` is now a reference to nothing.

The problem is caused by returning a reference to a parameter. This creates a dangling reference.

Answer 23: The programmer did not put spaces in the output text for the line:

```
13    std::cout << "Twice" << number << "is" <<
14        (number *2) << '\n';
```

as a result, the output looks like

```
Twice5is10
```

What he should have written is:

```
std::cout << "Twice " << number << " is " <<
        (number *2) << '\n';
```
(spaces added)

Answer 24: This is a classic deadlock problem:

Process 1 requires resources #1 and #2.

Process 2 requires resources #2 and #1.

They get the resources in that order. Remember that thread switches can occur at any time.

So we have a race condition in which the following can occur:

1. Process 1 gets resource #1

2. Thread switch to process 2

3. Process 2 gets resource #2

4. Process 2 attempts to get resource #1

5. Resource #1 is unavailable, so the process sleeps until it is freed (keeping resource #2 locked while it works)

6. Thread switch to process 1

7. Process 1 attempts to get resource #2. It's locked, so the process sleeps until it is freed. (Resource #1 is kept locked in the meantime.)

The result is that process 1 is waiting for resource #2 while holding resource #1. It will not give up resource #1 until it gets resource #2.

Process 2 is waiting for resource #1 while holding resource #2. It will not give up resource #2 until it gets process #1.

Avoidance 4: Define locking order (for example, you must get the locks in the order #1, #2). Always use this locking order when getting multiple locks.

Alternate: When getting multiple locks, use the following algorithm:

1. Attempt to get all the locks (do not block if they are not available).

2. If you've got everything, then go on and do your job.

3. If you didn't get all the locks, free the ones you didn't get, sleep a while, and try again.

Answer 25: The problem is the statement:

```
if (n2 =! 0)
```

This is an assignment statement inside an `if`. If we rewrite the code to avoid the shortcut, we get the two statements.:

```
n2 = !0;
if (n2)
```

The use of the logical not in this context (`!0`) gives us a result of 1. So we always assign `n2` the value 1, then do the comparison and divide.

The `!=` was written backwards as `=!` thus giving us the surprise.

The statement should have read:

```
if (n2 != 0)
```

Answer 26: The problem is:

```
diff[diff_index++] =
    array[i++] - array[i++];
```

This tells the compiler to:

1. Increment `i`

2. Use it to index array (first occurrence)

3. Increment `i`

4. Use it to index array (second occurrence)

5. Compute the difference

The problem is that steps 1-4 can occur in a different order:

1. Increment `i`

2. Increment `i`

3. Use it to index array (first occurrence)

4. Use it to index array (second occurrence)

Statements with many side effects give the C++ compiler latitude to screw things up.

Avoidance 5: Put side effects like `++` and `--` on lines by themselves.

Answer 27: The problem is that "1" is an integer. The number "3" is also an integer. So "1/3" is an integer divide.

Thus, the statement:

```
12    result = 1/3;    // Assign result something
```

does an integer divide of 1 by 3. Integer divides truncate the fractional part so the result is 0. The integer "0" is turned into floating-point and assigned result.

The programmer should have written this as:

```
12    result = 1.0 / 3.0;// Assign result something
```

Answer 28: The scanf function is extremely tricky to use. In this program the statement:

```
22        scanf("%c %d", &oper, &value);
```

gets a character and a integer. The next time scanf is called, it will read another character and integer. So what's the next character? Let's look at the sample run:

```
% calc
Enter operator and value:+ 5
Total: 5
Enter operator and value:+ 10
Bad operator entered
Total: 5
Enter operator and value:Bad operator entered
Total: 5
Enter operator and value:q
Bad operator entered
Total: 5
Enter operator and value:q
```

The first line we type is:

```
+ 5
```

After the first scanf call, the input pointer is position just before the newline just after the 5. The next scanf tries to read the operator and gets the newline. It keeps reading and sees a + instead of a number. The result is a lot of confusion.

Avoidance 6: The scanf function is tricky to get right. But I have a simple way of dealing with this problem: I never use it. Instead I always use a combination of fgets and sscanf instead.

```
fgets(line, sizeof(line), stdin);
sscanf(line, "%c %d", &operator, &value);
```

Answer 29: The preprocessor does not understand C++ syntax. When we define TOTAL to be 37 + 33, it is literally 37 + 33 and not 70.

The AREA macro is defined as:

```
37 + 33 * 10
```

Operator precedence takes over and gives us the wrong answer.

Avoidance 7: Use constants instead of defined macros whenever possible.

Avoidance 8: Put parenthesis around all #defines that define anything other than a simple number.

Example:

```
// Total top size
#define TOP_TOTAL (TOP_PART1 + TOP_PART2)
```

Answer 30: The problem is that the function is returning a reference to a local variable. This is a bad thing because the local variable is destroyed by the return; the reference is what is called a *dangling reference*. It's referring to something that is no longer there.

When we try to print the string that is no longer there, we run into trouble.

Avoidance 9: Do not return references to local variables.

Answer 31: The problem is that the else clause goes with the nearest if. The properly indented code looks like:

```
23 if (balance < 0)
24     if (balance < - (100*DOLLAR))
25         cout << "Credit " << -balance << endl;
26     else
27         cout << "Debt " << balance << endl;
```

This is not what the programmer intented. What he wanted to do was:

```
if (balance < 0) {
    if (balance < - (100*DOLLAR))
        cout << "Credit " << -balance << endl;
} else
    cout << "Debt " << balance << endl;
```

Avoidance 10: Use {} around statements under the control of an if, for, while, or other control statement if there is more than one statement conditional control.

(That's a fancy way of saying: Don't write code like this.)

Bonus question: This fixes most of the problems, but there's still a bug in this program. What is it? (Next Hint 112. Answer 38.)

Answer 32: The problem is that memory is allocated in the constructor and never freed.

Avoidance 11: Always **delete** in the destructor what you **new** in the constructor.

This rule was not followed, so every time we created a stack some of the heap permanently went away.

Answer 33: The program prints:

```
First: John
Last:  Smith
Hello: John
  Smith
```

The problem is that fgets gets a line including the newline. So when the first name is read, it's read as John\n. The same thing happens with Smith, and the result is our funny output.

Answer 34: There is a extra semicolon at the end of the for statement:

```
for (index = 1; index <= 10; ++index);
```

This means that the for controls absolutely nothing. Properly indented the program is:

```
for (index = 1; index <= 10; ++index);
std::cout << index << " squared " <<
    (index * index) << '\n';
```

or if we add a little commenting this looks like:

```
for (index - 1; index <= 10; ++index)
    /* Do nothing */;
std::cout << index << " squared " <<
    (index * index) << '\n';
```

From this we can see that the std::cout line is not inside the for loop.

Answer 35: The problem is that we declared a local variable named remove. There is a standard function named remove as well. Our local variable hid the function for the scope of the local variable.

That scope ended at the end of the first if on line 15.

The next statement:

```
16    if (remove) {
```

checks to see if the address of the function remove is non-zero and executes the next statement if it is.

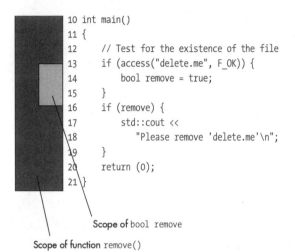

```
10 int main()
11 {
12    // Test for the existence of the file
13    if (access("delete.me", F_OK)) {
14        bool remove = true;
15    }
16    if (remove) {
17        std::cout <<
18            "Please remove 'delete.me'\n";
19    }
20    return (0);
21 }
```

Scope of bool remove

Scope of function remove()

Avoidance 12: Avoid hidden variables.

Answer 36: The problem is that the string we return is defined as:

```
15    // The name we are generating
16    std::string name;
```

This is a local variable. The subroutine returns a reference to this string. But because it's a local variable, it's destroyed at the end of the function. That means when we use the result, the variable holding the result has been destroyed.

Answer 37: The problem is that the backslash character is used as an escape character. So \n is newline. \new is <newline>ew.

So the string \root\new\table decodes as

```
"<return>oot<newline>ew<tab>able"
```

What the programmer really wanted was:

```
const char name[] = "\\root\\new\\table";  // DOS path
```

Ironically, this rule does not apply to #include file names so

```
#include "\usr\include\table.h"
```

works and is correct.

Answer 38: The problem is the statement:

```
if (balance < 0)
```

This is used to check to see if the customer owes the company something. Thus, the customer can see a message like:

```
You owe 0.
```

NOTE *This actually happened to one person. He got a bill for $0.00. He called up the company, they apologized, and the next month he got a bill for $0.00. This continued for many months. Each time he called the company, they would apologize and tell him they would fix the problem, but nothing would happen.*

He even got charged a late fee of 5%. This brought his bill up to $0.00.

Finally, he sent them a check for $0.00.

That week he got a nasty phone call from his bank. "Why did you write out such a check?" they demanded to know.

It seems that the check crashed its computer system. So the check was bounced, and the next week he received a bill for $0.00.

Answer 39: The problem is that the optimizer is smart. It sees that we are computing the result of

```
factor1 * factor2;
```

inside the for loop. The answer won't change if we move this to outside the for loop, but things will go quicker. So the optimized version of this program does the multiply only one time:

```
17    int register1 = factor1 * factor2;
18    // We know that 1863 multiplies
19    // delay the proper amount
20    for (i = 0; i < 1863; ++i)
21    {
22        result = register1;
23    }
```

To fix this problem we need to declare our factor volatile.

```
 1 /**********************************************
 2 * bit_delay -- Delay one bit time for        *
 3 *       serial output.                        *
 4 *                                             *
 5 * Note: This function is highly system        *
 6 *       dependent.  If you change the         *
 7 *       processor or clock it will go bad.    *
 8 **********************************************/
 9 void bit_delay(void)
10 {
```

```
11    int i;      // Loop counter
12    volatile int result;// Result of the multiply
13
14    // Factors for multiplication
15    volatile int factor1 = 12;
16    volatile int factor2 = 34;
17
18    // We know that 1863 multiples delay
19    // the proper amount
20    for (i = 0; i < 1863; ++i)
21    {
22        result = factor1 * factor2;
23    }
24 }
```

It's things like this that make embedded programming so simple.

Answer 40: The problem is that ostream is passed as "pass by value". You can't copy stream variables. (If you did it would mean that the system would have to make a copy of the file.) The parameter should be changed to a "pass by reference" parameter:

```
void print_msg_one(
    // File to write the message to
    class ostream &out_file,

    // Where to send it
    const char msg[]
)
```

Answer 41: The problem is the statement:

```
strcat(file_name, '/');
```

The strcat function takes two strings as arguments. In this example, we've given it a string and a character. Because there are no prototypes, C can't do parameter checking; the incorrect parameter is passed to strcat, which gets very confused.

Avoidance 13: All functions should be explicitly declared. Never let C declare them implicitly. Make sure you include the headers that define the prototypes for all the functions that you use.

Answer 42: A signed one-bit number can have one of two values: 0 and -1.

The statement:

```
printer_status.online = 1;
```

fails because the one-bit-wide field can't hold the value 1. (So it overflows and assigns the variable the value -1!) The result is that the next statement:

```
if (printer_status == 1)
```

fails.

Avoidance 14: Single bit fields should be `unsigned`.

Answer 43: On MS-DOS you'll get something like:

```
The answer is 4C:>#
(# is the cursor)
```

On UNIX you might get something like:

```
The answer is 4$ #
```

The problem is that the programmer did not add an end of line at the end of the `std::cout` statement. The result is that the program runs, outputs a statement, and exists leaving the cursor positioned at the end of a line. The command processor then runs and outputs its prompt (C:> for MS-DOS, $ for UNIX) right next to the program's output.

What the programmer should have written is:

```
std::cout << "The answer is " << result << '\n';
```

Answer 44: Commas can be used to separate C++ statements. It's used like:

```
if (x)
    std::cout << "X set. Clearing\n", x = 0;
```

(Don't program likc this, please!)

The statment

```
one_million = 1,000,000;
```

is the same as:

```
one_million = 1,
000,
000;
```

or

```
one_million = 1;
000;
000;
```

From this, we can see why we get 1 as out output.

Answer 45: The problem is that the expression ch+1 is an integer (value 66). C++ detects this and calls the std::cout.operator <<(int) function and outputs an integer.

What the programer should have written is:

```
std::cout << static_cast<char>(ch+1);
std::cout << static_cast<char>(ch+2);
```

Answer 46: The output is:

```
The double of 1 is 2
The double of 2 is 3
The double of 3 is 4
The double of 4 is 5
The double of 5 is 6
```

The reason is that DOUBLE(i+1) expands to:

```
(i+1 * 2)
```

When C++ sees this, it multiplies 1 by 2 and adds i. This result is not what the programmer intended.

Avoidance 15: Use **inline** functions instead of macros whenever possible.

Avoidance 16: Always put () around the parameters of macros. Example:

```
#define DOUBLE(x) ((x) * 2)
```

Answer 47: The statement:

```
if (amount = 0)
```

assigns 0 to amount, then compares the result to see if it's not zero. It is zero, so the else clause is executed.

The programmer should have written the statement as:

```
if (amount == 0)
```

NOTE *One of the most rewarding experiences I had when I was teaching programming was when I met a student about two months after the class had finished.*

"Steve," he said. "I have to tell you that during the class I thought you were going a bit overboard about this '=' vs. '==' stuff — until yesterday. You see, I wrote my first real program and guess what mistake I made?"

Answer 48: Use the statement:

```
i = 3 - i;
```

NOTE *This algorithm was first found lurking in an article as an example of how not to do the job. The author's "ideal" way of doing things was to use the following code:*

```
switch (i) {
    case 1
```

```
            i = 2;
            break;
        case 2:
            i = 1;
            break;
        default:
            std::cerr << "Error: i is not 1 or 2\n";
            exit (99)
    }
```

The point the author was trying to make was that you should check for illegal values in your code.

Sharp-eyed readers may notice that there's a syntax error in this code. There was a similar problem in the "ideal" solution in the original article. In other words, the code the author presented as "ideal" wouldn't work.

Answer 49: The problem is that C++'s operator precedence is not what the programmer thought it was. The + operator comes before << so

```
    y = x<<2 + 1;
```

gets parsed as:

```
    y = x << (2+1);
```

The result is 1<<4 or 8.

Avoidance 17: Use the simple C++ precedence rules:

1. *, / and % come before + and -.
2. Put () around everything else.

Answer 50: It prints

```
Hello
Hello
```

The problem is that when the fork occurs, there is data in the printf buffer. The fork creates two copies of the process and two copies of the data in the printf buffer. Thus, when the buffer is flushed later (in both processes) we get a Hello from each of them.

Answer 51: The programmer never bothered to initialize sum. You can't count on a uninitialized value containing anything. So sum may start out at 0, 5190, 123, 5, or something else.

What the programmer should have written is:

```
9    int sum = 0;
```

Answer 52: The problem is the line

```
flags |= CD_SIGNAL;
```

This operation is not protected against thread switches. On a complex instruction machine, the assembly code for this looks like:

```
; 80x86 assembly
orb $2,flags
```

Thread switches occur only on an instruction boundary. So this operation cannot be interrupted on the 80x86 machine family.

But on a RISC machine such as a Sparc, the code looks a little different:

```
1. sethi %hi(flags),%o0     ; Get the address of the flags in %o0,%o1
2. sethi %hi(flags),%o1
3. ld [%o1+%lo(flags)],%o2 ;%o2 = contents of the variable flags
4. or %o2,2,%o1             ;%o1 = The results of seeting the flag
5. st %o1,[%o0+%lo(flags)] ;Store results in %o0
```

So now the C++ statement is interruptible. In particular, the following can happen:

1. The program runs and completes instruction 3. At this point, the value of flags is in register %o2.
2. A thread switch occurs.
3. The other process modifies flags.
4. The thread switches back.
5. The old value of flags is in register %o2.
6. The bit is set, and the result is stored. Because this contained the old value of flags, any changes made in the other thread are discarded accidently.

The solution to this problem is to use locks to prevent a task switch from occurring during the statement.

Answer 53: The statement:

```
48              printf("%o\t", matrix[row][col]);
```

prints the answer in octal. The programmer made an error and put %o where he wanted %d. The result is that the numbers are correct, just in the wrong base.

Answer 54: The problem is that you can't represent 1/3 exactly in floating-point. Let's see what happens when we add the numbers in decimal.

```
1/3 = 0.33333
1/3 = 0.33333
1/3 = 0.33333
------------
      0.99999
```

Because of the roundoff error, the result is not 1.

Remember that when using floating-point, the numbers are not exact.

Answer 55: The problem is that we throw an exception in a destructor.

When the program reaches the line:

```
if (i3 < 0)
    throw (problem("Bad data"));
```

the exception code takes charge. It destroys all the local variables. That includes the variable a_stack.

When a_stack is destroyed, the destructor is called:

```
~stack(void) {
    if (count != 0) {
        throw (problem("Stack not empty"));
    }
}
```

The destructor throws an exception. C++ does not like it when you throw an exception in an exception. When that happens the program calls the terminate() function.

If you want to catch the second exception and other similar exception problems, use the standard function set_terminate to establish a function to take care of unexpected problems.

Avoidance 18: Don't throw exceptions in destructors.

Answer 56: The problem is that the redefined new function is implemented incorrectly. The programmer assumed that when a person does a

```
new fast_bit_array
```

the size of the allocated object is sizeof(fast_bit_array). This is not true when fast_bit_array is used as a base class. In this case, the size of the allocated memory is the size of the derived class safe_bit_array, which is bigger than fast_bit_array, thus resulting in memory confusion.

Avoidance 19: Don't define your own operator new function unless you're sure what you're doing. If you are sure you know what you're doing, make sure you're really really sure. Even then don't do it unless it's absolutely necessary.

Answer 57: The problem is that there are two variable declarations:

File: main.cpp

```
int value = 20;
```

File: check.cpp

```
int value = 30;
```

That means that the value is set to 20 or 30. But which one? The result is compiler-dependent. If you want value to be local to the files in which they are declared, you need to declare them static:

File: main.cpp

```
static int value = 20;
```

File: check.cpp

```
static int value = 30;
```

Or better yet, give them two different names.

Answer 58: According to the C++ standard, once you define a derived class member function with the same name as a base class's member function, all member functions of that name are hidden:

So `der::print_it(float)` hides both `base::print_it(float)` and `base::print_it(int)`.

When we call `print_it(2)` C++ looks for a version of `print_it` it can use. The only visible `print_it` is `der::print_it(float)`. C++ would rather have a function that takes **int** as its argument, but it knows how to turn an **int** into a **float**, so it promotes 2 to 2.0 and uses `der::print_it(float)`.

Answer 59: The problem is that we didn't define a copy constructor. When that happens, C++ defines one for you and generally does a bad job of it.

The copy constructor is defined as:

```
var_array(const var_array &other) {
    data = other.data;
    size = other.size;
}
```

The copy constructor is called to create a copy of `an_array` for the function `store_it`. The pointer to the data is copied.

When `var_array::~var_array` is called at the end of `pushy`, it returns the data to the heap.

When `var_array::~var_array` is called at the end of `main`, it returns the same data to heap. Because we delete the same memory twice, the result is a corrupt heap.

Avoidance 20: Always declare a copy constructor in some way or other.

The three major was are:

1. Implicitly declare it.

2. If you never want anyone to be able to call it, declare it private:

```
private:
    var_array (const var_array &);
    // No one can copy var_arrays
```

3. If the default works, use the comment:

```
// Copy Constructor defaults
```

in your program. That way you tell people reading your code that you thought about it and know that the C++ default will not be a problem.

Answer 60: The programmer has a very bad habit of not closing files after opening them. Pretty soon the maximum number of files are opened and the system won't let him open any more.

Closes needed to be added at key points in the code:

```
int fd = open(cur_ent->d_name, O_RDONLY);
if (fd < 0)
    continue;    // Can't get the file so try again

int magic;       // The file's magic number
int read_size = read(fd, &magic, sizeof(magic));
if (read_size != sizeof(magic)) {
    close(fd);    // <---- added
    continue;
}

if (magic == MAGIC) {
    close(fd);       // <---- added
    return (cur_ent->d_name);
}

close(fd);        // <---- added
```

Also the programmer uses `opendir` to open a directory. He never closes it. So a `closedir` is needed.

```
void scan_dir(
    const char dir_name[]    // Directory name to use
)
{
    DIR *dir_info = opendir(dir_name);
    if (dir_info == NULL)
        return;
    chdir(dir_name);

    while (1) {
        char *name = next_file(dir_info);

        if (name == NULL)
            break;
```

```
                    std::cout << "Found: " << name << '\n';
              }
              closedir(dir_info);      // <---- added
        }
```

Answer 61: The problem is that the statement:

```
5 const char *volatile in_port_ptr =
6         (char *)0xFFFFFFE0;
```

tells C++ that the *pointer* is volatile. The data being pointed to is not volatile. The result is that the optimizer still optimizes us out of existence. The solution is to place the volatile where it modifies the data being pointed to. We also have added a const to the declaration to make sure that the pointer can't be modified. The resulting declarations are:

```
4 // Input register
5 volatile char *const in_port_ptr =
6         (char *)0xFFFFFFE0;
7
8 // Output register
10 volatile char *const out_port_ptr =
11         (char *)0xFFFFFFE1;
```

This tells C++:

• in_port_ptr is a const pointer and cannot be modified.

• *in_port_ptr is a volatile char whose value can be changed outside the normal C++ programming rules.

Answer 62: The problem is that the comment:

```
10     base = 5;   /* Set the base of the triangle
```

does not contain a close comment. So it continues engulfing the statement below it:

```
10     base = 5;   /* Set the base of the triangle
11     height = 2; /* Initialize the height */
```

From this it's easy to see why height was not set.

Answer 63: The problem is that getchar returns an int. We are assigning it to a character. Some systems treat characters as unsigned characters. The result is that when we get EOF (-1) the system assigns

```
ch = (unsigned char)(-1)
```

or ch = 0xFF. It then compares the 0xFF to -1 (they are not the same) and does not exit the loop.

This program is also a stylistic disaster. The goal of every C++ programmer should be writing a clear program. This program was written to be compact. A much better program is:

```
1  /**********************************************
2   * copy -- Copy stdin to stdout.             *
3   **********************************************/
4  #include <stdio.h>
5
6  int main()
7  {
8
9      while (1) {
10     {
11         int ch; // Character to copy
12
13         ch = getchar();
14
15         if (ch == EOF)
16             break;
17
18         putchar(ch);
19     }
20     return (0);
21 }
```

Answer 64: The output is:

```
Name (a): /var/tmp/tmp.2
Name (b): /var/tmp/tmp.2
```

The reason for this is that although we have two pointers, they both point to one variable name. When tmp_name is called the first time:

```
a_name --> name = "/var/tmp/tmp.1"
```

After the second call:

```
b_name --> name = "/var/tmp/tmp.2"
```

But a_name also points to name so:

```
a_name --> name = "/var/tmp/tmp.2"
b_name --> name = "/var/tmp/tmp.2"
```

The second call overwrote storage that was being used to hold the result of the first call.

One solution to this is to copy the string after each call or to have the caller provide his own character array for name storage.

Another solution is to use C++ style strings that handle their own memory allocation.

Answer 65: Every `put` is followed by a `flush`. This means that a system call is made for each character output. System calls are expensive and take up a lot of CPU time.

In other words, although the I/O library is designed for buffered I/O, the excessive `flush` calls for it to do unbuffered I/O one character at a time.

We need to flush at the end of each block to make sure that the remote system receives a full block. That's *block*, not *character*, so we can speed up the system by moving the `flush` down to after the block is sent:

```
for (i = 0; i < BLOCK_SIZE; ++i) {
    int ch;

    ch = in_file.get();
    serial_out.put(ch);
}
serial_out.fflush();
```

Answer 66: The `setjmp` marks a location in the code. The `longjmp` call jumps to it. It jumps directly to it, it does not pass go, it does not collect $200. It also skips all the destructors for all the variables on the stack. In this case, because the destructor for `std::string` returns the memory allocated for the string, we have a memory leak.

That's because the `setjmp` and `longjmp` functions are C functions that should not be used in C++.

Avoidance 21: Do not use `setjmp` and `longjmp` in a C++ program. Use exceptions instead.

Answer 67: In the default case:

```
defualt:
    std::cout << i << " is not prime\n";
    break;
```

The "default" keyword is misspelled. The result is that the C++ compiler thinks that "defualt" is a `goto` label.

Answer 68: The `printf` function buffers its output. It won't actually write anything until the buffer gets full or a newline is sent.

So the program hits the `printf`, the "Starting" message goes into the buffer and not to the screen, and the function average is executed and gets a divide by zero error.

The result is that the "Starting" message is lost, making us think that average was never called.

The solution to this problem is to flush the buffer explicitly after the starting message:

```
        printf("Starting....");
        fflush(stdout);
```

WARNING *The rules for when a buffer gets flushed change depending on the type of file being written. The rules are:*

1. If `stdout` or `stderr` are being written to the screen then the output is buffered until:

   a. When a line is written.

   b. When `stdin` is read.

   c. When the buffer gets full.

2. If `stdout` or `stderr` are being written to a disk then the output is buffered until:

   a. When the buffer gets full.

(These are the rules you'll probably find on your system. The actual rules are system-dependent.)

Answer 69: The problem is the programmer wrote:

```
std::cout << "Hello World!/n";
```

instead of:

```
std::cout << "Hello World!\n";
```

so the output is literally:

```
Hello World/n
```

Answer 70: The problem is the statement:

```
54    while (
55        (std::strcmp(cur_cmd->cmd, cmd) != 0) &&
56        cur_cmd != NULL)
```

The statement checks the data pointed to by `cur_cmd->cmd`, then checks to see if `cur_cmd->cmd` is valid. On some systems, dereferencing NULL (which we do if we are at the end of the list) causes core dumps.

On MS-DOS and other brain-damaged systems, there is no memory protection, so dereferencing NULL is allowed, although you get strange results. Microsoft Windows fixed this, and dereferencing a NULL pointer will result in a General Protection Fault (GPF).

The loop should be written:

```
while (
    (cur_cmd != NULL) &&
    (std::strcmp(cur_cmd->cmd, cmd) != 0))
```

But even this is tricky. The statement depends on the C++ standard being correctly implemented. That C++ standard states that for && the first part is evaluated. If the first term is false, the second term is skipped. Just to be safe, it's better to write this as:

```
while (1) {
    if (cur_cmd == NULL)
        break;
    if (std::strcmp(cur_cmd->cmd, cmd) == 0)
        break;
```

Answer 71:

1. Alignment

Some machines require that long integer values line up on a 2-byte or 4-byte boundary. Some do not. C++ will insert padding in the structure to make things line up.

So on one machine, the structure will be:

```
struct data {
    char flag;        // 1 byte
    long int value;   // 4 bytes
};
```

for a total of 5 bytes. While on another it may be:

```
struct data {
    char flag;        // 1 byte
    char pad[3];      // 3 bytes (automatic padding)
    long int value;   // 4 bytes
};
```

for a total of 8 bytes.

2. Byte order

Some machines write out long integers using the byte order ABCD. Others use DCBA. This prevents things from being portable.

3. Integer size

The 64-bit machines are coming. That means that on some systems a long int is 64 bits, not 32.

Answer 72: We have an array of a derived class called safe_stack. In C++, you can use a base class pointer (stack*) to point to a derived class (safe_stack). The system will see only the base part of the object, but you can still point to it.

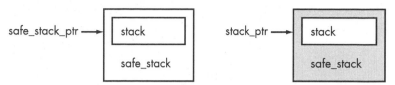

Now a pointer can point to a single instance of a class or an array of objects.

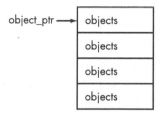

So we have the following two rules:

    1. A base pointer can point to a derived object.

    2. An object pointer can point to an array of objects.

From this, we can conclude:

    1. A base pointer can point to an array of derived objects.

That's wrong.

The problem is that an array of derived objects is not the same as an array of base objects.

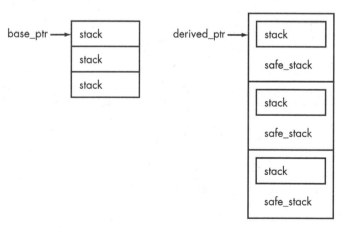

So if we take a base pointer and point it a derived array, the memory layout will be wrong.

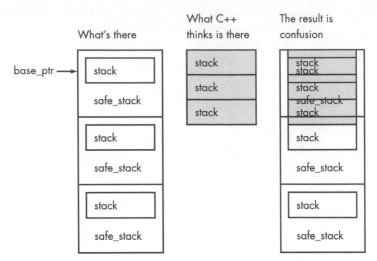

What's there | What C++ thinks is there | The result is confusion

Avoidance 22: Use the STL vector template instead of an array. It avoids a lot of problems.

Avoidance 23: Do not pass base-class arrays as parameters.

Answer 73: The problem is how the compiler generates machine code for program.

The statement:

```
if (number1 + number2 == number1)
```

generates something like:

```
movefp_0, number1
add fp_0, number2
movefp_1, number1
fcmpfp_0, fp_1
jump_zero  out_of_the_while
```

In this example fp_0 and fp_1 are floating-point registers. In floating-point coprocessors, the registers have the largest precision available. So in this case, while the numbers may be only 32-bit, the floating-point processor does things in 80 bits, resulting in a high precision being reported.

This sort of problem occurs on most machines with a floating-point processor. On the other hand, if you have an old machine that uses software to do the floating-point, you'll probably get the right answer. That's because, in general, software floating-point uses only enough bits to do the work.

To fix the program, we need to turn the main loop into:

```
while (1)
{
```

```
// Volatile keeps the optimizer from
// putting the result in a register
volatile float result;

result = number1 + number2;
if (result == number1)
    break;
```

Answer 74: The problem is that the words are stored in the input file in alphabetical order and the tree is unbalanced. Thus, when words are inserted the following data structure is built up:

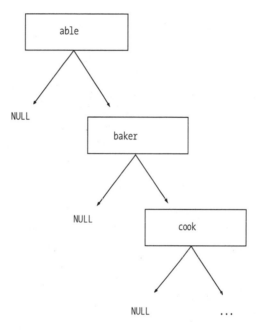

The result is that we have a linked list, not a tree. Words are added to the end of the linked list (expensive), and lookups are done by linear search (also expensive).

A balanced binary tree would solve this problem.

Answer 75: The problem is that we have in our code the statement:

```
an_array = an_array;
```

This is disguised as:

```
82    to_array = from_array;
```

The `operator =` function deletes the data of the destination array. That's fine except that the source array is the same stack, so its data gets destroyed, too.

The answer is to check explicitly for self-assignment in the operator = function:

```
      array & operator = (const arrary &old_array) {
   if (this == &old_array)
                  return;
```

Avoidance 24: The operator = function should check for self-assignment.

Answer 76: The problem is that strcmp returns 0 if the strings are equal and non-zero otherwise. That means that if you have the statement:

```
      if (strcmp(x,y))
```

The if will execute only if the strings are *not* equal.

Avoidance 25: Use

```
      if (strmp(x,y) != 0)
```

to test if two strings are equal. It's clearer than if (strcmp(x,y), and it works.

Avoidance 26: Whenever possible, use the C++ string class instead of the old C style strings. That way you can use the relational operators (<,>, ==, etc.) instead of strcmp.

Answer 77: The problem is the code:

```
   while (first != NULL) {
      delete first;
      first = first->next;
   }
```

It deletes data, then uses it. After things are deleted, they really should go away.

Avoidance 27: Always set a pointer to NULL after delete or free.

When the code is written with a little bit of added protection, the problem is obvious:

```
      delete first
      first = NULL;
      first = first->next;
```

Also, because of the added protection of setting first to NULL, if we do attempt to use the pointer, we will abort in a well-defined manner (on most systems).

Answer 78: The types of the variables are:

sam is a character pointer (char *).

joe is a character (char).

The declaration, after the preprocessor gets through with it results in:

```
   char * sam, joe;
```

Avoidance 28: Use `typedef` to define new types, not `#define`.

Answer 79: C++ has no ** operator. (At least for integers.) So (12 ** 2) is an invalid construct.

The trouble is that this bad syntax is hidden in a preprocessor macro that's not expanded until line 16. That's why line 16 is the one with the syntax error.

Avoidance 29: Use `const` instead of preprocessor macros whenever possible. The statement:

```
const int GROSS = (12 ** 2);
```

would still generate an error message, but at least the line number would be right.

Answer 80: The problem is that the result of a comparison is an integer 1 or 0. So the expression:

```
if (a > b > c)
```

becomes

```
if ((a > b) > c)
```

Because a is greater than b, the result of a > b is 1, so we now have

```
if (1 > c)
```

which is false, so the else clause is executed.

Answer 81: The programmer suspects that something funny is happening when data item #500 is read. He wants to put a breakpoint right before this item is read.

The trouble is that if he puts a breakpoint at the top of get_data, he will have to do 500 debugger continue commands before he reaches the point he wants.

So he puts his breakpoint at the line:

```
seq = seq;
```

NOTE *The fancier debuggers allow the user to set a skip count to skip the first x number of breakpoint stops. Our friendly programmer doesn't have such a nice tool.*

Answer 82: The programmer used semicolons to end the `#define` declaration. Because the preprocessor is rather literal about things, the semicolon becomes part of the text. The result is that USABLE is defined as:

```
8.5; -1.0;;
```

The initialization of text_width now becomes

```
double text_width = 8.5; -1.0;;
```

or, properly indented,

```
        double text_width = 8.5;
        -1.0;

        ;
```

From this we can see our problem.

Avoidance 30: Use const instead of #define whenever possible.

Answer 83: The problem is the buffer is a local variable. That means that it goes away at the end of the function call. Unfortunately, printf doesn't know this, so it will still stuff data into it afterwards.

The

```
        printf("That's all\n");
```

will still try to use the local variable.

To fix this problem declare the buffer as static:

```
        static char buffer[BUFSIZ];
```

Answer 84: The problem is the optimizer. The optimizer knows that the variable debugging is zero. It's always zero.

Now that we know that, let's take a look at the statement:

```
        if (debugging)
```

This is always false, because debugging is always zero. So this block is never executed. That means that we can optimize the code:

```
13      if (debugging)
14      {
15          dump_variables();
16      }
```

into the statement:

```
        // Nothing
```

Now let's look at the number of times debugging is used. It's initialized on line 11 and used on line 13. Line 13 is optimized out, so debugging is never used. If a variable is never used, it can be optimized out.

The result is an optimized program that looks like:

```
 9 void do_work()
10 {
11      // Declaration optimized out
12
13      // Block optimized out
14      //
15      //
16      // End of block that was removed
17      // Do real work
18 }
```

Now our programmer wanted to use the debugging variable to help him debug things. The trouble is there is no debugging variable after optimization.

The problem is that C++ didn't know that the programmer was going to use magic (a debugger) to change variables behind its back. If you plan on doing something like this, you must tell the compiler. This is done by declaring the debugging variable volatile.

```
static volatile int debugging = 0;
```

The "volatile" keyword tells C++, "Something strange such as an interrupt routine, a debugger command, or something else may change this variable behind your back. You can make no assumptions about its value."

Answer 85: The printf statement:

```
11    printf("The answer is %d\n");
```

tells C to print an integer, but fails to supply one. The printf function doesn't know this, so it will take the next number off the stack (some random number) and print it.

What the programmer should have written is:

```
printf("The answer is %d\n", answer);
```

Answer 86: The problem is the use of matrix[1,2]. The comma operator in C++ merely returns the result of the second part. So the expression "1,2" tells C++ throw the first part (1) away and the value is 2. So matrix[1,2] is really matrix[2]. This is a pointer into an integer array, and C++ will treat it as a pointer for printing. That's why strange values get printed.

What the programmer really wanted is:

```
matrix[1][2]
```

Answer 87: The prefix version of ++ returns the number after incrementing. Thus

```
++++i;
```

tells C++ increment i, returns the result, then increments the variable i again.

The postfix version of ++ (i++) returns a copy of the variable, then increments it.

So

```
++++i
```

1. Tells C++ to make a copy of i (call it tmp_1)
2. Increments i
3. Does the rest of the work on tmp_1
4. Makes a copy of tmp_1 (call it tmp_2)
5. Increments tmp_2
6. Returns tmp_1 as the value of the expression

C++ won't let you get away with ++++ on integers. Only with some added class silliness can you get away with it.

Avoidance 31: Use ++ and -- singly.

Answer 88: The problem is the macro:

```
#define SQR(x) ((x) * (x))
```

when called with

```
SQR(++number)
```

This expands to

```
((++number) * (++number))
```

This increments number twice, instead of once as the programmer intended. What's worse, the compiler can make some decisions as to the order in which the various operations are done; therefore, the result of this expression is compiler-dependent.

Avoidance 32: Use **inline** functions instead of parameterized macros.

Avoidance 33: Put ++ and – on lines by themselves.

Answer 89: The optimizer knows that although the subroutine computes the value of result, it does nothing with it. So the program will work the same whether or not result is computed. Thus, the optimizer takes a look at the loop:

```
20      for (i = 0; i < 1863; ++i)
21      {
22          result = factor1 * factor2;
23      }
```

is optimized down:

```
20      for (i = 0; i < 1863; ++i)
21      {
22          /* Do nothing */;
23      }
```

Of course we don't need to do nothing 1,863 times, so this is optimized down to:

```
20      /* No loop needed */
21      {
22          /* Do nothing */;
23      }
```

This is about as optimized as you can get. The way to keep the optimizer from doing this to us is to declare the variable result is volatile. Program 110 shows what happens when you add this fix.

Answer 90: C++ uses zero-based indexing. So for `array[5]` the valid elements are:

array[0], array[1], array[2], array[3], array[4]

The programmer, however, uses the elements 1-5. There is no `array[5]`, so the program modifies random memory, causing the memory corruption.

That's why most C++ programs don't use statements like:

for (i = 1; i <= 5; ++i) {

Instead they count using:

for (i = 0; i < 5; ++i) {

Answer 91: The problem is that with the statement:

result=result/*divisor;   /* Do divide */;

the first /* (the one in the middle of the statement) starts a comment; it does not do a divide. So this statement is:

result = result   /* a very big comment */;

Avoidance 34: Put spaces around operators. It not only avoids problems but also makes the program easier to read.

result=result / *divisor;   /* Do divide */;

Answer 92: The problem is that a thread switch can occur at any time.

The writer will remove a character from the buffer when count > 0. The reader performs the two steps:

++count; // We've got a new character
*in_ptr = ch;// Store the character

But a thread switch can occur between these two steps.

Therefore, the following can happen:

reader:++count;// We've got a new character

thread switch to writer

writer: check count > 0 -- it is

writer: Get the character

thread switch to reader

reader: Put the character in the buffer AFTER writer has already read it.

A solution is to change the sequence of the steps

```
++count;   // We've got a new character
*in_ptr = ch;// Store the character
```

to

```
*in_ptr = ch;// Store the character
++count;   // We've got a new character
```

Depending on the sequence of instructions to protect shared data is difficult and tricky.

It is much better and simpler is to tell the task manager when you are doing a set of statements that can't be interrupted. In pthreads, this is done with a mutex lock:

```
pthread_mutex_lock(&buffer_mutex);


++count;
*in_ptr = ch;
++in_ptr;


pthread_mutex_unlock(&buffer_mutex);
```

Answer 93: Member variables are initialized in *declaration* order.

In this case, the statements:

```
) : width(i_width),
    height(i_height),
    area(width*height)
```

are executed in declaration order: 1) area, 2) width, 3) height. This means that area is initialized with undefined values of width and height, and then width and height are initialized.

Avoidance 35: Write constructors so that variables are initialized in the order in which they are declared. (If you don't do this, the compiler will do it for you and cause confusion.)

Avoidance 36: Never use member variables to initialize other member variables.

Answer 94: In K&R style functions, the parameter declarations come immediately *before* the first curly brace.

That means that the declaration:

```
int sum(i1, i2, i3)
{
```

declares three parameters of default (int) type. Anything after that is declared as a local variable.

In particular

```
int sum(i1, i2, i3)
{
    int i1;   /* Local variable, not parameter */
    int i2;   /* Local variable, not parameter */
    int i3;   /* Local variable, not parameter */
```

The result is instead of summing three parameters, the program adds three uninitialized local variables. No wonder we get a strange result.

Answer 95: The problem is the statement:

```
24    sscanf(line, "%c %d", oper, value);
```

The sscanf function takes pointers as its arguments. (Remember C doesn't check arguments for the correct type.) In this case, we gave sscanf a character and an integer. We should have given it a pointer to a character and a pointer to an integer:

```
24    sscanf(line, "%c %d", &oper, &value);
```

Answer 96: The program use raw I/O to do its work (using the read and write system calls). This program does one raw read and raw write for each character. Operating calls are expensive, and this program uses 2 (one read and one write) per byte copied.

To speed up the program, cut down on the operating system calls. This can be done two ways:

1. Use the buffered I/O system by making the input and output fstreams instead of file descriptors.

2. Read and write more than one character at a time.

Answer 97: The problem is the statement:

```
for (index = 0; string[index] != '\0'; ++index)
    /* do nothing */
return (index);
```

There is no semicolon after the /* do nothing */ statement.

The return is part of the for statement. The code should look like this after it is indented properly:

```
for (index = 0; string[index] != '\0'; ++index)
    /* do nothing */
    return (index);
```

From this code section we can see that the first time through, the for loop index will be zero and the return taken. That's why all the strings are of zero length.

What the programmer wanted was:

```
for (index = 0; string[index] != '\0'; ++index)
    /* do nothing */;
return (index);
```

Answer 98: The problem is that class is allocated not by the C++ new operator, but instead uses the old style C malloc operator. This creates the space for the class without calling the constructor.

Then just to add insult to injury, memset is called to zero the class.

```
result =
    (struct info *)malloc(sizeof(struct info));
memset(result, '\0', sizeof(result));
```

What the programmer should have written is:

```
result = new info;
```

NOTE *The author first found this problem in a large library he was trying to debug. Because of the large size of the library and the complexity of the mess, it took him a week to find the location of the malloc.*

Answer 99: The statement:

```
out_file << ch;
```

does not send a character to the output. Regardless of its name, the ch variable is of type integer. The result is that the integer is printed to the output. That's why the output file is full of integers.

This is the one case in which C++'s automatic type detection of output parameters gets in your way. The old C printf statement would handle things correctly like:

```
printf("%c", ch);
```

But with C++ you must cast to get the correct results in this case:

```
out_file << static_cast<char>(ch);
```

Answer 100: The program outputs:

```
First: second Second: second
```

The problem is that the readdir returns a pointer to static data. This data is owned by readdir and overwritten by subsequent calls.

So what happens is this: We call scan_dir and set first_ptr to point to the string first. That's what we want, but the array containing the name is static and when we call readdir again, it uses the same buffer to store the name second. So now first_ptr points to second, which is the cause of our trouble.

readdir function
(after second read)

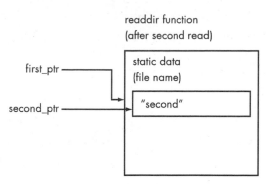

Answer 101: In the base class destructor, we call the function clear.

This function calls a pure virtual function, delete_data.

During destruction, the derived class gets deleted first. When the derived class goes, so does the definition of delete_data. Next, the base class destructor is called. In this case, our list class indirectly calls delete_data, which is pure virtual. Because there is no derived class, the runtime system causes the program to abort.

Avoidance 37: Do not call pure virtual functions from a constructor or destructor of an abstract class.

Answer 102: I expect the results to be:

```
First 1
First 1
First 1
Second 1
Second 2
Second 3
```

but the results are:

```
First 0
First 0
First 0
Second 0
Second 1
Second 2
```

The problem is the statement:

```
return (i++);
```

Now I *knew* that this added one to i and returned. The problem is that i++ is the value of i *before the increment*. So what the statement really does is:

1. Save the value of i.
2. Increment i.

3. Return the saved value.

So the lines:

```
i = 1;
return (i++);
```

cause a 1 to be returned, not a 2 as one might expect.

Avoidance 38: Put ++ and – on lines by themselves.

Answer 103: The problem is that on some systems, longs must align on a four-byte boundary. So let's take a look at our structure:

```
struct end_block_struct
{
    unsigned long int next_512_pos;    // [0123]
    unsigned char next_8k_pos1;        // [4]
    unsigned char next_8k_pos2;        // [5]

    unsigned long int prev_251_pos;    // [6789]
```

6 is not divisible by 4, so the compiler adds two padding bytes to make it jump to 8. So what we really have is:

```
struct end_block_struct
{
    unsigned long int next_512_pos;    // [0123]
    unsigned char next_8k_pos1;        // [4]
    unsigned char next_8k_pos2;        // [5]

    unsigned char pad1, pad2;          // [67]
    unsigned long int prev_251_pos;    // [89 10 11]
```

This is not what's indented.

Avoidance 39: Put statements like

```
assert(sizeof(end_block_struct) == 16);
```

in your code to catch compilers that cause this problem.

Another avoidance is to make every member of the structure a byte and assemble the short and long ints yourself. This is more work, however.

Answer 104: The zip code 44101 is too large for MS-DOS's 16-bit integer. The largest number a 16-bit integer can hold is 32,767. The result is that the number overflows into the sign bit, and things go wrong.

NOTE   *Win32 systems use 32-bit integers, so this problem does not occur on the current versions of Microsoft Windows.*

Answer 105: The ABORT macro is expanded into two statements. So the result of the `if` statement is:

```
if (value < 0)
    std::cerr << "Illegal root" << std::endl;exit (8);
```

or properly indented:

```
if (value < 0)
        std::cerr << "Illegal root" << std::endl;
exit (8);
```

From this output it's easy to see why we always exit.

Avoidance 40: Use inline functions instead of multistatement macros.

```
inline void ABORT(const char msg[]) {
    std::cerr << msg << std::endl;
    exit(8);
}
```

Avoidance 41: If you must use multistatement macros, enclose them in curly braces:

```
#define ABORT(msg) \
    {std::cerr << msg << std::endl;exit(8);}
```

Answer 106: The problem is the statement:

```
char prev_ch = '\0';
```

Because `prev_ch` is an automatic variable, this variable is created and initialized at the beginning of each loop. This means for the first `if` the variable `prev_ch` will always hold `'\0'` and we'll never match double letters.

Answer 107: This program makes the big mistake of using floating-point for money. Floating-point numbers may not be exact. When adding up a lot of floating-point numbers, some errors may creep in.

The solution is to change the program to store money not in fractional dollars but as an integer number of cents.

Avoidance 42: Don't use floating-point for money or anything else you want represented exactly.

Answer 108: The printf call prints whatever string you give it. If you add 1 to a character string, you get the string minus the first character.

So:

```
printf("-xxx") prints -xxx
printf("-xxx" + 1) prints xxx
```

The expression `((flags & 0x4) != 0)` returns a 0 or 1 depending on whether the bit is set.

The programmer is printing -word if the bit is set ("-word" + 0). The output is word if it is clear ("-word" + 1).

NOTE *If you are going to be this clever in your code, comment it to tell the maintenance programmers how smart you are.*

Answer 109: The problem is the operator = function. It's defined as:

```
trouble operator = (const trouble &i_trouble)
{
    std::cout << "= operator called\n";
    data = i_trouble.data;
    return (*this);
}
```

The return value of this function is the class trouble. But there's a problem. Because the function does not return a reference, a copy of the variable has to be made. That means that the copy constructor has to be called. This calls the operator = function, which does the return, calling the copy constructor and so on.

The solution is to have the operator = function return a reference to the class:

```
trouble& operator = (const trouble &i_trouble)
```

Answer 110: The initialization of log_file can call new. Of course, our new new uses the log_file, so the log_file may be used before it gets constructed, confusing the whole mess.

Avoidance 43: Don't redefine the global new and delete unless you know what you are doing. Really know what you are doing. Even then don't do it.

Answer 111: The problem is that the initialization order of global variable is not guaranteed. In this case, a_var assumes that std::cout is initialized. That may not be the case.

Let's assume the worse and assume that the initialization order is a_var, std::cout. In that case, a_var is created. The constructor is called and output a message to std::cout. Because std::cout has not been created yet, things get very confused and the program crashes.

Answer 112: The problem is that MAX is defined to be literally the text "=10" That means that

```
for (counter =MAX; counter > 0; --counter)
```

expands to

```
for (counter ==10; counter > 0; --counter)
```

This does not initialize the counter (it merely compares counter to 10 and throws the result). Because the counter is not initialized we get a random number of greetings.

NOTE *The GNU preprocessor sticks spaces around macro expansions so that the GNU version of the expansions:*

```
for (counter = =10 ; counter > 0; --counter)
```

It's unfortunate that the good GNU technology is robbing us of the opportunity of debugging strangely failing programs.

Answer 113: The space after the name DOUBLE makes this macro a simple text replacement macro. Thus,

```
#define DOUBLE (value) ((value) + (value))
```

causes DOUBLE to be replaced with:

```
(value) ((value) + (value))
```

Literally!

This means that the line

```
std::cout << "Twice " << counter << " is " <<
    DOUBLE(counter) << '\n';
```

looks like:

```
std::cout << "Twice " << counter << " is " <<
    (value) ((value) + (value))(counter) << '\n';
```

(Indentation added.)

Solution: Define DOUBLE as

```
#define DOUBLE(value) ((value) + (value))
```

Avoidance 44: Use inline functions instead of parameterized macros whenever possible. Example:

```
inline DOUBLE(const int value) {
    return (value + value);
}
```

Answer 114: The problem is that the optimizer feels free to rewrite the code. Some optimizers will stick variables in registers to make the code go faster. For example, one optimized version of this program looks like:

```
1  /*********************************************
2   * sum -- Sum the sine of the numbers from 0 to *
3   *      0x3FFFFFFF.  Actually we don't care     *
4   *      about the answer, all we're trying to   *
5   *      do is create some sort of compute       *
6   *      bound job so that the status_monitor    *
7   *      can be demonstrated.                    *
8   *********************************************/
9  /* --- After the optimizer  --- */
10 /* --- gets through with it --- */
11 static void sum(void)
12 {
13     static double sum = 0;      /* Sum so far */
14     register int reg_counter = counter;
15
16     for (reg_counter = 0;
17          reg_counter < 0x3FFFFFF; ++reg_counter)
18     {
19         sum += sin(double(reg_counter));
20     }
21     printf("Total %f\n", sum);
22     counter = reg_counter;
23     exit (0);
24 }
```

From this, we can see that counter is updated only after the program finishes. If we try to examine it at any time in the other thread we die.

The solution it to declare the variable volatile:

```
volatile int counter;
```

Then the compiler will make no assumptions about what it can do about it regarding optimization, and will generate code that keeps counter is kept up-to-date.

Answer 115: I am trying to always make sure I delete the variable data before I overwrite it so I don't have a memory leak. I even delete it in the following code:

```
34         // Copy constructor
35         v_string(const v_string &old)
36         {
37             if (data != NULL)
38             {
```

```
39              delete[] data;
40              data = NULL;
41          }
42          data = strdup(old.data);
43      }
```

This is the copy constructor. The first thing it does is to see if `data` has anything in it and, if so, `delete` it. But what could `data` possibly have in it? We just created the class and haven't initialized it yet. So we are deleting a random pointer and as a result, crashing. Properly written our copy constructor should be:

```
34      // Copy constructor
35      v_string(const v_string &old):
36          data(strdup(old.data))
37      {}
```

THE BOOK OF WI-FI
Install, Configure, and Use 802.11b Wireless Networking

BY JOHN ROSS

A practical and plain English guide to a fun but tricky technology. Shows how to build and use wireless networks at home, at work, or in your neighborhood. Includes detailed information on setting up and configuring access points, network interface cards, cables and antennas, and wireless software. Also discusses how to secure your wireless access point with encryption, password protection, and virtual private networks (VPNs). Covers Windows, Macintosh, Linux, Unix, and PDAs. For beginners on up.

2003, 504 PP., $29.95 ($44.95 CDN)
ISBN 1-886411-45-X

STEAL THIS COMPUTER BOOK 3
What They Won't Tell You About the Internet

BY WALLACE WANG

This offbeat, non-technical book looks at what hackers do, how they do it, and how readers can protect themselves. The third edition of this bestseller adopts the same informative, irreverent, and entertaining style that made the first two editions a huge success. Thoroughly updated, this edition also covers rootkits, spyware, web bugs, identity theft, hacktivism, wireless hacking (wardriving), biometrics, and firewalls.

"If this book had a soundtrack, it'd be Lou Reed's Walk on the Wild Side.*"*
— InfoWorld

2003, 464 PP, $24.95 ($37.95 CDN)
ISBN 1-59327-000-3

UPDATES

Visit **http://www.nostarch.com/hownotc.htm** for updates, errata, and other information.

THE BOOK OF VISUAL STUDIO .NET
A Guide for Developers

BY ROBERT B. DUNAWAY

Surveys each .NET server and related technologies, with a focus on Visual
Studio 7 (VS7). Hands-on examples cover building forms, data retrieval,
moving to COM+, and implementing web services. Other key issues and
solutions include upgrading from Visual Basic, source control services,
and remoting.

"...a direct and accessible guide to learning the ins and outs of the various
tools applicable to Visual Studio .NET." — The Midwest Book Review

2002, 392 PP., $49.95 ($74.95 CDN)
ISBN 1-886411-96-7

THE BOOK OF SAX
The Simple API for XML

BY W. SCOTT MEANS AND MICHAEL A. BODIE

Includes everything XML and Java developers need to write SAX applications. Specific examples show how to use SAX to solve XML parsing
problems that are impractical to address with tree-based technologies —
including real-time parsing, very large documents, and high-performance
applications. The authors guide readers through the development of
picoSAX, a functioning SAX 2.0 XML parser.

"The Book of SAX delivers. Publisher No Starch Press concentrates on
accurate, straightforward, compact tutorials and references. SAX fits this
style well." — UNIX Review

2002, 312 PP., $29.95 ($44.95 CDN)
ISBN 1-886411-77-8

Phone:

1 (800) 420-7240 OR
(415) 863-9900
MONDAY THROUGH FRIDAY,
9 A.M. TO 5 P.M. (PST)

Fax:

(415) 863-9950
24 HOURS A DAY,
7 DAYS A WEEK

Email:

SALES@NOSTARCH.COM

Web:

HTTP://WWW.NOSTARCH.COM

Mail:

NO STARCH PRESS
555 DE HARO STREET, SUITE 250
SAN FRANCISCO, CA 94107
USA

Distributed in the U.S. by Publishers Group West